HOW NEVADA'S DUAL-MONETARY ... FINANCE THE RE-ACTIVATION OF NEVADA ... NEVADA'S CITIZENS FROM ...

By JAMES RAY HOUSTON

The founding fathers of this great nation were very much aware of the fact that Federal Government has the power to cause a run-away inflation of the currency. The reason for this awareness was the fact that before the signing of the Constitution in 1787, the founding fathers experienced run-away inflation after the Continental Congress created the Continental Currency. The reason that the Continental Currency lost its purchasing power was because it was a *Fiat* Currency (meaning paper money that could not be redeemed for silver or gold). The term, "not worth a Continental Damn!" comes from this tragic period of our nation's history.

Thousands of Americans lost their wealth and life savings during this devastating period of inflation. Without a stable currency with which to facilitate the exchange of commerce, the American economy ground to a complete HALT. Only after the introduction of hard currency (silver), was the economy revived. Only then did American money gain and enjoy the stability and the reputation which would finally establish it as the strongest and safest money in the entire world.

As a safe-guard to the people and the states against the possibility of government caused run-away inflation, the authors of the Constitution placed a special provision in Article 1, Section 10 of the Constitution, which in effect authorizes the states and the people, respectively, to use gold and silver as "a tender in payment of debts."

At this point in the history of our Nation nearly everyone recognizes that run-away inflation is a distinct possibility. It is the duty of the Governor of this state to protect the economy of this state from any possible danger. Run-away inflation is a great danger to Nevada's economy. Yet no contingency plan exists. Put another way, if a possibility of rain exists, it is only prudent to have an umbrella. The "umbrella" in this case, is an alternate form of currency better known as The Dual-Monetary System.

THE DUAL-MONETARY SYSTEM

The system is so simple and uncomplicated, that it is difficult to understand why it has not been enacted before now. The state simply creates silver and gold certificates which can be redeemed for a specific weight (gram — 31 to an ounce) of gold and silver. For example: a 100 gram silver certificate could be redeemed at any time for 100 grams of silver.

The state sells these certificates as "Inflation Hedges" through brokers, banks and gold and silver exchanges, in the same manner as municipal bonds are now sold. The certificates would be desired by investors all over the world who wish to own silver or gold without the "hassle" of actual possession of the metal bars. As the state sells the certificates, it buys the silver and gold to back them up. The certificates are sold at what ever the market price is at the time of purchase.

No one is forced to do business in silver or gold grams, unless they desire to do so.

In addition to fulfilling the need of an alternate medium of exchange, the system has 2 major advantages for the people of Nevada:

1. TOTAL FINANCING OF THE REACTIVATION OF NEVADA MINES

Thousands of Nevada's gold and silver mines have been inactive for the last 50 years. In the last four years silver has increased in price from $1.30 an ounce to $4.00. In the same time gold has tripled in price from $50 per ounce to $150 per ounce. It is widely predicted that both of these metals will double in price again within 24 months. Even at current prices, hundreds of mines are profitable to mine at this time. The reason that mines are not opening up right now is the fact that start up costs average 2 million dollars and no one has stepped forward with this needed financing. However, with the Dual-Monetary System the state could profitably perform this function. Providing that mine owners could prove to the state that ore reserves were ample to guarantee future delivery, the state could purchase silver or gold from the mine owners in advance.

For example: Suppose you owned a silver mining property, and you could prove to the state that your mine would be profitable to reactivate.

However, you needed 2 million dollars in start up capital to build your mill, construct your smelting operation, hire your work force, block your ore, etc. The state would purchase 2 million dollars worth of silver on contract and funds would be made available in progress payments — similar to current bank construction loans and under state supervision from the mine.

After you delivered 2 million dollars worth of silver to the state, you would be free and clear to continue to produce silver from your property.

Should the experts determine that there was a risk factor involved as to the ability of you to deliver, the purchase price of the silver purchased would be discounted to compensate for the risk taken.

In return for providing start up capital, the state would require that you sign an agreement to sell up to one half of your silver production to the state (at its option) at a 20% discount to market price.

This provision would create a very unique opportunity for the state to profit from the Dual-Monetary System. Since the state sells the certificates at 100% of market price, and buys gold and silver at only 80% of market price, the state would make an administrative profit of 20% of sales. This little fact creates an exciting benefit for Nevada's citizens.

2. EXEMPTING NEVADA CITIZENS FROM PERSONAL TAXATION

The state of Nevada presently extracts 54.4 million dollars annually from people in the form of sales tax. In addition, the people of Nevada pay approximately 30 million annually in the form of personal property taxes (taxes on automobiles, furniture, boats and other personal property).

If I am elected Governor I will personally see to it that the 100 million plus dollar profit realized from the 20% administrative profit of the Dual-Monetary System will be used to exempt our citizens from these burdensome and unnecessary taxes.

JAMES RAY HOUSTON

Countdown To

DEPRESSION

by

James Ray Houston

DEDICATION

This Book Is Dedicated to Four of
America's Greatest Living Patriots

W. CLEON SKOUSEN

ROBERT PRESTON

EZRA TAFT BENSON

GARY ALLEN

CREDITS — Many thanks to I. Ellessac for the research
and editing of the manuscript. And a special thanks to my lovely wife, Barbara, who
was an inspiration to me in writing this
book.

Published by
Sun-Star Publishing
1506 Las Vegas Blvd. So.
Las Vegas, Nevada 89104

TABLE OF CONTENTS

To The Reader:

Today, more than ever before, there is a need in America for Patriots such as James Houston, the author of this book. We must take a stand for freedom, now!

It is only through efforts like "Countdown To Depression" and other serious attempts to expose this very real conspiracy, that we may survive. It is only through exposure that these shadowy figures can be weeded out of the primroses and then, effectively neutralized. It is because of this dedication to truth that our national enemies will attempt to make this book a non-book. You can make sure that their efforts are not successful. We believe that Americans should always have a choice about all matters affecting them and the future of the country. Your individual actions are both critical and important to the survival of that traditional selection process. The choice is yours.

Gary Allen

ECONOMIC FUTURE SHOCK

These ten economic disasters will occur in the very near future:

1.) Individual income tax information will be opened for all to see.
2.) The Federal Reserve System will fail to protect bank-held money.
3.) There will be a panic and most banks will fail again.
4.) Unemployment figures will skyrocket monthly.
5.) Paper currency will become valueless in the market-place being replaced by gold and silver as the medium of exchange.
6.) The Social Security system will fold from a lack of funds.
7.) There will be a crushing depression regardless of the new President's inspirational political rhetoric.
8.) Pension plans will lose from 70% to 90% of their invested value in a pension trust fund scandal.
9.) The era of the credit card will collapse and the public will rebel against the mega-computer invasion of individual privacy that the credit card is responsible for, across America.
10.) There will be much protest and urban unrest as the have-nots of all races fight for survival.

During this entire period of trouble and trial for our nation, the international socialist/communist conspiracy will be gloating over the success of their programs to destroy the middle-class American in their efforts to force our country into a one-world form of government. On the following pages I will outline how these agents of confusion and dismay have effectively infiltrated every branch of our economic, educational, and governmental life, causing among other things, the financial woes we now suffer. Why do I say these things? Am I simply another prophet of doom hammering away at a now familiar theme to sell books? I invite you to read on, and then, you can judge. What I have found in my search for answers is a serious situation which many citizens seemingly refuse to recognize, in spite of the obvious.

In setting about the task of compiling a manuscript such as this, which deals with the economic, hence political, realities of 1974, I do not have to be a seer, a fortune-teller, nor a prestigious financial prognosticator to readily be able to glean some glaring trends which become very obvious as one peruses the many facts available to all. As unpleasant as many of these trends may be, the truth is the light, and this light will keep us free.

The first trend is the fact that the governmental invasion of individual rights in the area of financial information, will soon reach the saturation point. Every corner merchant and/or fly - by - night operator will be able to secure a full financial disclosure on any individual's economic status, including the supposedly confidential information contained on one's last income tax form. They can do this simply by joining, at a very nominal fee, a computer hook-up established especially for this purpose.

It is a fact that right now, at the very moment that you are reading this page, there is an agreement between a growing number of states and counties throughout the country, and the Internal Revenue Service, giving them complete and total access to the information contained in your 1973 tax return. Already there are numerous reports of corrupt local officials peddling this information to interested private firms, for a fee, of course. Who is doing the buying? For starters think about insurance companies looking for prospects, detective firms seeking information for lawsuits, credit agencies wanting financial information for client firms, and home improvement companies seeking selective solicitation.* The rights of financial privacy for the individual are fast fading in the face of these many assaults from the big government of the 1970's.

Another trend that is obvious is the vulnerability of the Federal Reserve System. This weakness will be proven very soon, in the wake of a run on small banks. The real victim of this vulnerability is the average depositor. Most average depositors ($1,000.00 to $10,000.00) feel very secure in the promise and propaganda of the Federal Deposit Insurance Corporation (FDIC). The FDIC promises to guarantee all deposits up to $10,000.00. The truth and the problem is that the FDIC can only make good on 1.2% of the total amount of bank deposits today. That leaves a 98.8% of all current American savers high and dry, with no real security once a pay-off period begins. When the failures start, the sham of security will end.

I predict that there will be massive bank failures, initially in the smaller, less secure banks. It is certain that the depositors will once again feel the burden of an inflation/depression cycle.

Let me also get on the record as stating that we are *now* in a depression. How long and how severe depends to a great extent upon what measures are now taken by an enlightened public. This book is part of an effort to make the depression less severe. Regardless of all of the rhetoric espoused by President Ford, the years of federal mismanagement are now about to take their terrible toll. The chickens are about to come home to roost, and the eggs they shall lay will include widespread unemployment, lean and hard times, the worst depression in our nation's history, and most probably a prolonged period of economic readjustment. Nixonomics and all of its federal predecessors have freely danced to the tunes of the Keynesian pipers, and now we must pay the bill for their economic indiscretions.

Moderates, liberals, conservatives, and all other political species must now meet the responsibility which was caused by the indiscreet printing of inflationary paper currency with no traditional metal (silver or gold) backing. Many decades ago President Franklin D. Roosevelt started borrowing against the future and we have now reached the point of no return in that reckless policy. The future is *now*. Our national IOU's are now due and payable. The situation is tragic.

Perhaps even more tragic is this next trend statement.

9

It is a fact that millions of America's senior citizens are going to soon find themselves drifting about with even less financial stability than they now have. This is because they will be without even the minimal support of their Social Security payments. What would make me say such a horrible thing? I say it simply because it is the truth, and we had better face it and start devising some alternatives or we will have to face the mass suffering of these helpless millions.

It is a fact that in 1935 the myth of social security began. Considering the ever spiraling costs of living combined with the ever increasing number of persons annually becoming eligible for social security benefits, it doesn't take a genius to see that the bubble soon must burst. When the political-waste bonanza of social security was dreamed up, our country had many million fewer citizens. These millions less people pooled their money in the social security bank against the future. As more and more persons took the benefits, more and more money was needed. It did not take many years for the saturation point to be reached.

Add to these woes the occasional cost-of-living increases Congress has voted to the benefits, and perhaps it may dawn on you, too, that we have long since been taking out more than we are putting into the fund. Every new citizen who applies for benefits now strains the faltering reserves left in this national retirement pension fund, reserves built by our parents and ourselves. Some day soon the well will run dry. This will be heightened by fewer and fewer people employed, because of the depressed economy. So, with more demanding benefits and fewer putting in, the unfortunate truth is that the funds simply will not be there.

Private pension plans and personal savings programs are the victims of the rampant inflation we suffer and endure today. In the beginning, the pension plans were set up to insure that a given amount of money was set aside monthly for the worker's retirement needs. Let us say that the amount was $50.00 per month, including the company's share, and expected to reap a monthly net, twenty years later, of, say, $85.00 per month. This increase was expected through investments and the interest on the principal. If the worker joined the plan in 1953, he has now had a year of trying to make $85.00 a month stretch to cover the fast-rising costs of food alone. Of course we know that it is next to impossible to try and live off of that small amount in 1974. There just isn't enough for just the basic survival needs of today. That's a fact.

Savings accounts, started during the same period of time in the fifties, have now declined in value at such a rapid rate, according to the dictates of our shrinking dollar, that as much as 60% of their original planned value is lost for the saver. What looked like a comfortable nest egg a few decades ago is now pitifully inadequate to meet the ever-rising costs of living today.

Many of the major union and private trust funds are invested in stocks and in the bank-loan programs available today. When the inevitable happens and the current non-money-money (paper bills) lose all hope of retaining any value in the public marketplace, these funds and invested pension trusts will suffer staggering losses. The money troubles we read about daily in Europe and Asia are closely tied into our own monetary fortunes. The Wall Street interests and the money professionals in London and Rome have woven a network of international monetary intrigue. At this point in history, both London and Rome stand on the verge of bankruptcy. If Wall Street's fate is intertwined with these international financiers, can the downfall of Wall Street be far behind?

The financial empire of the Rothschilds and their fiscal cohorts worked diligently and with resolve to make sure that America's economic fate was closely related to that of Europe. Because of these influences, it is a fact that the American economy is now based upon a concept of spending too much money to chase too few goods. In other words, in true Keynesian fashion, excess paper (non-money-money) currency has been made available to the public in order to support the illusion of perpetual good times, while the supply and demand pressures of a natural

11

market have always been suppressed to try and hide the real shortages and recessions. Much of the more-than-ample currency supply was based solely on the easy credit policies of the credit card era. This concept was supported by the federal government.

So we were spending mountains of unreal money, which we really did not have in our treasury, to get everything we could possibly want or dream of, and more. We are coming to the end of a long period during which it was best for the buyer to beware. It had been the sellers' market. The fantasy had to come to an end. We had constructed a credit pyramid, going deeper and deeper in debt as a result of easy credit. All such non-metal based credit pyramids must eventually collapse and the time for this one's collapse is now upon us. Adding insult to injury, on top of the huge public gross national product, which was largely established through the liberal use of easy credit terms, the federal government kept pace with the unreal spending orgy by creating the terrible 480-plus billion dollar deficit. Just the interest alone on this gigantic debt, is more than the entire national budget was just a few years ago. The legislators in Washington, are spending money like drunken sailors in some exotic far-away port. Unlike the fabled sailors, when this orgy is over, we will still have to face the mountain of debt they have caused us to suffer.

Finally, most of the lending economists have now conceded that we indeed must have a continuing inflation or face a steep rise in unemployment. Unemployment is a dirty word to politicians, so many of them close their eyes to the reality of hyper-inflation. Inflation, when uncontrolled (as in Germany during the twenties) is much like a giant forest fire — feeding on itself and all in its path, growing eventually into an awesome fire storm which destroys everything in its path. A fire storm feeds on oxygen and flammable materials. Inflation feeds on easy credit, and a greed for higher prices and higher profits.

Inflationary influence on retail prices brings about inflationary labor wage demands, which in turn cause

12

inflationary costs in services and the skilled fields of labor they represent. All of this brings about the still higher costs of retail products, to keep pace with the times. So the vicious circle is complete and the fiscal fire storm rages on and on, with production, labor, management, and the professionals all clamoring for their share of the big-money pie. Each in turn, accusing the other of being the villian in the matter.

It is rather evident that we cannot fight a raging fiscal fire storm with a mere garden hose or a small fire extinguisher. Rather, we need to seriously consider some bold and extraordinary measures to contain this holocaust. This is what our current crop of political leaders is either unwilling or unable to do. It is politically unpopular to advocate measures which are sure to lead to higher unemployment and massive business failures. But it is unreal to try and ignore the obvious and to continue to try to live in this socialistically-inspired Keynesian nightmare which has brought us to the very brink of national economic ruin. We must be mature enough to face up to the facts that are controlling our economic lives today or we leave ourselves open to repeat the run - away inflation which led to the power grab by Hitler in Germany during the twenties. Who among us is willing to look forward to the spector of paying six million dollars for a loaf of bread or perhaps as much as seventeen million dollars for a house note or rent? If we don't come up with some answers very soon, that is where our inflation spiral is going to lead us, and much sooner than most of us want to admit.

What America needs is a new brand of grass-roots leadership — a bold, I-Love-America kind of leadership which is dedicated to the continued greatness of our country. Feature writer Herbert Rowan of the Washington Post wrote an article during the summer of 1974 which stated unequivocally that many responsible American and international bankers now openly admit that they fear an irreversable money panic and the resultant depression that this would cause. What Mr. Rowan would not state, but what is also true, is that the coming depression will be more severe and of greater endurance than the great depression of the thirties.

Among the new words being coined to describe our economic condition today is the word stagflation. It means that our economy is stagnant, while the cost of every product and service is in a continuous state of runaway inflation. Our current politicians are afraid to take the moves necessary to stop this or to change things. My roots are deep in the soil of America, but I am of the new bold breed who fear not the imaginative changes we must institute to save our country. For people of bold persuasion, there is a cure for this stagflation. It is a system I call the Dual Monetary System.

The fires of inflation do not have to form into the spectacle of the all-consuming fire-storm and destroy our economy and our nation. Facing the truth and implementing bold plans for economic stability are the answers to many of our current problems. I sincerely hope that when you finish reading this book, you will see what needs to be done, and why, in order to save our capitalistic-oriented democratic republic and the way of life I am sure that we prefer over all the others now known in the world. I hope that this book both informs and inspires you to do what must be done to accomplish these goals.

JAMES RAY HOUSTON

September 1974

---

* *Newsweek* — Periscope, 5 August, 1974

CHAPTER ONE

"THE ROOT OF ALL EVIL"

Almost all Americans are in some manner familiar with the crash of '29 and the resultant decade of depression that followed that event. But how many of these same aware people know that at the beginning of our great nation, equal financial misfortunes almost made our young American dream a nightmare? I am going to start my efforts at that point in history, when General Washington and the valiant founders of this republic were engaged in the bitter life-and-death struggle on the frigid plains of Trenton and Valley Forge, and the newly-born American economy struggled for survival in the seats of commerce and industry.

It is a fact that in August of 1775, the Continental Congress did issue the first Continental currency. This early Continental currency was paper money that was not backed by silver or gold (or any precious metal). It was in fact, nothing more than a system of national IOUs, intended to be available for redemption by silver and gold in some future promised day (eight to thirteen years thence). Within the first year of issue, the Continental currency had been devalued in the nation's marketplaces by a minimum of fifty percent (50%).

To correct this problem, a bureaucracy was formed and called the "Council of Safety." These Councils (each state had its Council) and the Continental Congress then took that first step down the supposedly simplistic road to problem-solving — the socialist pie-in-the-sky promise of salvation — they (the Congress and the Councils) interferred with the free enterprise of the citizens' marketplace. The Councils and the Congress decreed price controls over goods and services for the good of the national economy (does that sound familiar?) and further imposed severe jail sentences and the confiscation of goods

15

for anyone who realistically admitted that the Continental paper money had in reality depreciated, or for anyone caught hoarding food and/or goods. So now you can see, there is an historic precedent for the establishing of federal price and wage controls and the freezes that the Nixon administration caused us to suffer. The federal government imposed the same unworkable restrictions in our early beginnings.

Like the recent price control laws, the first ones did not accomplish the stated goals either. What happened was that the controls created shortages of salt, grain, and many other items during the 1770's. Additionally, by the early spring of 1779, there was a state of general starvation in some of the Northeastern cities that had been prosperous just a few years before. The fortunes of the Continental currency held even worse news.

The Continental dollar was first printed and issued in the late summer months of 1775. A year later it was valued at only half that amount. Four years later it had further devalued in the marketplace to a point where it was worth only five percent (5%) of the printed valuation of the note. At this point the Continental Congress was finally forced to admit the errors of the attempt to pawn the worthless paper on the public and to declare bankruptcy.

The Continental currency, at the time of bankruptcy, was being exchanged at a rate of five-hundred Continental dollars to one silver dollar. The valued silver dollars had a firm value throughout the original colonies and this value extended to the international marketplace. In other words, the holders of the silver dollars had a monetary unit that had a dependable and proven value. On the other hand the Continentals had little or no value to anyone, anywhere. As a result of this condition, much of the commerce of the time had to be carried on by means of barter and many service-oriented people had no products to barter. This situation caused much unneeded suffering and the Northeastern starvation.

The Congress, seeking to enforce stop-gap measures to halt the rampant deflation of the Continentals, issued *new* non-silver and non-gold backed paper money. This new money was exchangeable at a rate of twenty old dollars to one of the new dollar bills. But once again, with no substantial metal-monetary-standard-value to back up the valueless paper, within a matter of a few months, the new currency had devalued by fifty percent (50%).

Finally, in 1792, after the Articles of Confederation had also failed to meet the needs of our new nation, and the all-new Constitution had created the new Congress, metal (silver), a monetary-standard-valued currency was introduced to save our economy. Only then did American money gain and enjoy the stability and the reputation which would finally establish it as the strongest and safest money in the entire world. That was a reputation that we enjoyed for many, many years, until new international forces started effectively undermining our once strong silver and gold reserves.

So the die was cast. Our government tried at the very beginning of our great nation, to regulate our free enterprise system. There are a great many well-documented works on the early attempts of these beginnings of governmental intervention into the private sector of our economy. I strongly suggest that the reader study the classic, "You Can Profit From A Monetary Crisis," by Harry Browne (1), especially noting the material in Part 11, "The Nature Of The Crisis," chapter 14 (page #99).

Moving ahead almost a hundred years, we will find that the tragedy of the Civil War allowed further inroads into federal control of the economy and into the private lives of the American citizen. One of the major seizures of personal liberty during this period was the landmark National Banking Act, which effectively ended all private control of American banks up to today. Adding to this insult was the injury of the government-issued U.S. Notes in 1862. Like the Continentals of a hundred years before, these U.S. Notes had no silver backing and no real value. Just one year later these bogus bills had driven all the real money (silver and gold) into a state of hoarded hiding. See how the more things change, the more they

17

are the same? Today many citizens keep their silver and gold off the marketplace, with much the same concerns that the citizen of the 1860's did. Within four (4) years (1867) retail prices on all goods and services had doubled. By 1873 the worst depression in the young Republic's history decended upon the economy-weary population. This depressed economy drug on and on until 1879, when President U. S. Grant by the use of his veto prevented Congress from authorizing the printing of more of the worthless inflationary currency.

During the early 1900's the federal government continued a stealthy march toward socialistic centralization of power by passing such incentive crushing measures as the Income Tax Amendment and the Federal Reserve Act (during 1913). We now fully understand the insidious omni-power which both of these seemingly innocent and benevolent acts of federal protection now casts over all American citizen's lives. But they were sold to our parents and grandparents as security-minded and safe acts to help the government guard our rights and our private lives. Nothing could be further from the truth. The wages of the ever-increasing bureaucracy is paid with the money derived from the income taxes we are now forced, under penalty of law to pay. That same bureaucracy spends much of the time and effort they expend in the planning and execution of plans to take away more and more of our individual liberties. The Federal Reserve Act is an example of early-day big-brotherism at its finest. The best federal government we could possibly have would be the least amount of federal government. A prime solution to many of our problems would be the decentralization of much of the federal bureaucracy.

Made bold by their successes in the Income Tax and Banking fields, the international monopolists decided to push their gains even further. The one-world power-brokers did not like our traditional conservative-isolationist positions internationally. In order to make us a part of the larger world, as they desired, we had to become more involved in the affairs of the world. Our historic stance had been a hands-off attitude concerning other nations' affairs. In order to get us involved, the one-world boys created a few 'incidents' for our benefit and then ballyhooed them all out of proportion to their real importance. Suddenly, because of these 'incidents' we looked up and were involved in the first World War. This involvement was continued and expanded upon, until now, in the 1970's, we can sadly point to the fact that we are the international guardians of all socialist and intra-national aggressions, the never-ending source of economic well-being for the rest of the world, the so-called peacemaker (?), the world developer, the international standard bearer of morals, the universal space researcher, and the generally accepted rich uncle to the entire galaxy (if the one-worlders can find a way to get their hands on the rest of the galaxy).

The early 1900's (1900-1928) saw the newly created Federal Reserve System (which was formed to end the local banking panics which in turn were caused by the earlier National Banking Act of President Lincoln's time) become responsible for a dizzying rate of uniform inflation (as opposed to segmented localized inflation) throughout America. By 1928 this run-away inflation imperiled the federal gold supply, so the economic federal managers felt compelled to deflate.

This deflation triggered the stock market crash of '29 and an honest-to-goodness, no-holds-barred depression enveloped the land for the next decade. The Federal Reserve Act has been hailed as depression proof. History has proven that it cansed the markets reassertion to the falsely supported price controls of inflation, and this caused a gigantic crash — a coast-to-coast crash that most probably could not have occurred without the meddling and the intervention of this so-called fool-proof Federal Reserve System.

Each succeeding administration since the 1920's, both Republican and Democrat, has faithfully promised in their campaign rhetoric to cut deeply into the rampant and entrenched bureaucracy, and then to return the nation to fiscal sanity. And each President, bar none, has then blissfully ignored that promise to the people, when safely entrenched in the highest office of the land. But still an ever hopeful electorate continues to cast their votes for a stability which vanishes in the reality of politics. Bureaucrats are, after all, vote-casting and vote-getting spheres of influence. Not only do succeeding administrations build larger and larger bureautic bases of power, civil-service frankensteins, if you will, but they continually sponsor more and more legislative programs which further extend executive powers over the private sector of the American way of life.

There it is, a thumbnail sketch of the historic pattern of economic bumbling by the federal government and some of the many big-brother-type fiscal policies they have traditionally embraced. In case you are one of the millions who assume that the shaky economic conditions of today are unique and unusual in the annals of American history, I hope these facts have enlightened you to the truth of the past. Rest assured that it is only the resiliency and the creative instincts which have allowed us to endure and survive our bureaucratic mismanagement of the past two centuries. Have hope, however, because it is this self-same toughness and our fabled American will to overcome, no matter how high the obstacles, which will see us through this current crisis, also.

Survival means awareness and the very fact that you are reading this book shows there is a degree of curiosity and awareness within. You join the elite group who must rally behind that awareness, to save our nation from the forces which threaten to envelop us. In your awareness you must also realize that you are in the minority. This aware minority must then find the means to awaken the vast majority of our relatives, friends, and neighbors who are still blissfully unaware.

We must make them see and understand the deadly danger which daily stalks our nation. If we fail in this task, soon, we may become the most efficient and knowledgeable slaves of this country. It is our duty to make these others understand that the dangers I have outlined are real and that the very high stakes are our way of life and that the game is being played with a deadly earnestness. We really do not have a choice, it is either stand up to the sinister forces who plot our overthrow or to surrender to them!!! Like my ancestor, Sam Houston, I cannot face the shame of surrender.

(1) "You Can Profit From A Monetary Crisis," Harry Browne, Macmillan, $8.95.

CHAPTER TWO

"THE SEED"

John Ruskin (1819-1900) was the son of a wealthy English wine merchant. He was widely traveled and well educated. He conceived and propagated a scheme of cooperative socialism. The scheme failed but the idea was firmly implanted in the fertile minds of some of his students, and they were the heirs to British aristocracy.

Ruskin's ideas were inspired by "Plato's Republic," and he talked feverishly about a ruling class with a powerful army to enforce that power. Ruskin advocated the use of force to wipe out any opposition to his plan, and he envisioned a society that was completely subservient to that force. Professor Kenneth Clark (1) wrote that Ruskin foresaw, " . . . that the state must take control of the means of producion and distribution, and organize them for the good of the community as a whole . . . his continual aim was to show the superiority of some men to others . . ." Ruskin had a dim view of democracy and it is interesting to note that the peasant communes of China today are an exact duplication of what he outlined in his model social and industrial movement. Ruskin's ideal society eliminated marriage and the institution of the family, with the children that resulted from the promiscuous unions belonging to and being raised by the state. He further believed that inferior and crippled children must be destroyed by the state.

In order to more fully understand this deceit and chicanery as dreamt up by this source of our misery, we fully recommend your reading Professor Clark's vital study for in-depth explanations of such things as Ruskin's 'Gold, Silver and Copper' soul theory of superiority/inferiority. These were explanations that Ruskin himself admittedly did not really believe in, but which he stoutly professed while in public. Information on the book is given at the end of this chapter.

One of the undergraduates at Oxford at the time of Ruskin's preachments was Cecil Rhodes (1853-1902), later famed as the exploiter of South African gold and diamonds (in partnership with one of the Rohtschild's and others — the DeBeers empire). Rhodes was so infected with the sensational impact of Ruskin, that he copied his entire inaugural lecture at Oxford in longhand. Rhodes rose in political power, becoming the prime minister of the Cape Colony (1890-1896) and a multi-millionaire, earning in excess of five million dollars annually. He devoted most of the prestige and power of his office and much of his lifetime income to the mysterious devotion that he held for Ruskin and his teachings. He totally believed Ruskin when he spoke of "Oxford undergraduates as members of the privileged ruling class." They were, Ruskin said, "Possessors of a magnificent tradition of education, beauty, rule of law, freedom, decency, and self-discipline." Ruskin advocated that these traditions must be spread to the masses of the world or ultimately be lost by the privileged rulers.

Cecil Rhodes accepted this concept lock, stock and barrel. He devoted the rest of his life, after Oxford, to the propagation of Ruskin's world federation ideas (one-world-ism). It was also in this light that Rhodes left part of his immense diamond-and gold-based fortune (DeBeers of South Africa) to perpetuate the world-famous Rhodes scholarships at Oxford University. As a current point of interest, it is enlightening to note how many of the individuals selected as the two-hundred probable leaders in the future, are Rhodes scholars. Check that fact out, count them (2). This curious fact is of particular significance when one realizzes that one of the major purposes of these scholarships is to spread Ruskin's one-world ideas throughout the English-speaking world. It is equally obvious that the future leadership of the 'Ruskin-theory' is selected from the ranks of these Rhodes scholars, to a great extent.

"Among Ruskin's most devoted disciples at Oxford were . . . Arnold Toynbee, Alfred (Lord) Milner, Arthur Glazebrook, George (Sir) Parkin, Philip Lyttleton Gell, Henry (Sir) Birchenough . . . A similar group of disciples grew at Cambridge University. These included Reginald Baliol (Lord) Brett, John B. (Sir) Seely, Albert (Lord) Grey, and Edmond Garrett. Both of these groups devoted the rest of their lives to the fulfillment and extension of Ruskin's ideas." (3).

One of England's most successful journalists, William T. Stead (1840-1912), brought both of these groups (Oxford and Cambridge) together under Rhodes' influence and guidance. He (Rhodes) immediately established the secret organization that he had been dreaming of and scheming for far more than sixteen years previous. The organization was officially established on 5 February, 1891.

Rhodes was the leader of this secret society. The executive committee included Stead, Lord Esher Brett and Milner. The inner circle, known as the "Circle of Initiates" included Lord Balfour, Sir Harry Johnson, Lord Rothschild (that name, somehow, seems to crop up in all money or power control schemes), Lord Grey, and others. The outer circle was known as the "Association of Helpers" and it is still extremely active, right now, this very day, now operating under the hush-hush name of "The Round Table Organization." The Round Table Organization is best known by the modern day name of "The Bilderberg Group." This round-table organization functions in many countries internationally, including the United States and Great Britain. The members of this group keep in close contact with each other by personal correspondence and by frequent visits to each other. This personal contact is abetted by a quarterly magazine, "The Round Table," which was founded in 1910 and largely supported by one Sir Bailey's money. In 1919 the group founded the "Royal Institute of International Affairs," with the financial help of Sir Bailey, again, this time

24

joined with financial help by the Astor family (from both the U.S. and England).

This institute was a part of an international (naturally) structure of similar organizations. One, known as the Institute of Pacific Relations, was set up in twelve different countries, with each of these countries having a stake in the Institute by dint of the fact that they each held colonial territories in the Pacific area. Each of these twelve units existed on an interlocking basis with the local Round Table and with the Royal Institute of International Affairs in the same country. In the United States, this institute is known as the Council on Foreign Relations. Whatever else you do as a result of reading this book, retain that name in your mind because it is far more important to the affairs of your daily lives than you may think at first glance. I will show that almost everything that happens in America today, on an official level, had its beginnings within the walls of this supersecret organization. It (the Council) is headquartered " . . . on the west side of fashionable Park Avenue at 68th Street (in New York City); There sit two handsome buildings across the way from each other. One is the Soviet Embassy. Directly opposite, on the southwest corner, is the Council on Foreign Relations — probably one of the most influential semi-public organizations in the field of foreign policy (4).

Just as Ruskin was the original source for this international one-world intrigue, so it is that the Council on Foreign Relations is the planning and strategy headquarters for contemporary plots against our freedoms. They must be exposed as such before it is too late to stop the plotting. It is of further interest for the reader to pay attention to the long list of influential Americans who are now members or alumni of this Council. The list reads like a "Who's Who" in American Education, Finance, Commerce, Politics, Industry, and Foreign Relations. In other words, in a very real sense they have been running the show. At the end of this chapter I am going to list just a few of these names to make you understand just how serious the situation is. I am not going to mention the associations, companies, and affiliations of the few that I mention, but you can easily find out who and what they are by taking this list to your nearest library and browsing through a few "Who's Whos" for just a short time. The list includes names of influence from 1915 until today.

Easily recognizable among the list are some of the well-known names of the rich and the super-rich, the highest elected officials, the publishers of many great and highly influential American newspapers and the heads of some giant publishing firms, the leaders of many of our best-known institutions of higher learning, not to mention the captains of industry and the governmental movers and shakers of prime importance. A still closer look at the political luminaries reveals that among this elusive cadre of persons who would rule the world, are several American Ambassadors, a head of the Federal Reserve Board, and one of the Atomic Energy Commission, several directors of Federal agencies, several heads of our intelligence-gathering agencies (and who do you think they are loyal to?), some of our most important economic advisors, and at least two recent Secretaries of State.

Are you still complacent and apathetic? I have named the names of some of the most powerful and the most influential public figures during the past seven decades at the end of this chapter, many of whom have been exposed time after time as those agents devoted to the disciplines which espouse ending the American way of life. As imperfect as it may be, the America we know and live in today is head and shoulders above all those forms of government that these deceivers and cheats would like to sell us into. They are not interested in our freedom and they are counting on our apathy. They are only interested in their own selfish goals — power, nothing else.

These conspirers do not dare bring their true aims and goals into the glare of daylight and offer the American public a chance to express their feelings on the matter in a national referendum because they know that we would overwhelmingly reject such a brazen scheme to deny us our freedoms. So instead of being above board, they hold secret meetings throughout the globe and at such meetings, plan the constant little withdrawals of our American liberties, such as the scheme of the highway/expressway-limited-access idea, as will be shown to you in the postscript of this book.

How many readers are aware that as recently as April of 1974, just one such secret meeting was held in the French resort area of Megeve. Prince Bernhard of the Netherlands is the present day Chairman of the secret group, as he has been for the past twenty (20) years. This German-born consort of the Dutch Queen, demands and gains the attendance of such international figures as our recently installed President — Gerald R. Ford (can you imagine how many of his moves will be dictated by his allegiance to the Round Table Group?) — as well as Helmut Schmidt, Dean Rusk, Christian Herter, Thomas Dewey, Edward Heath, Amintone Fanfani, and of course — Henry Kissinger.

All of the above mentioned leaders have attended recent secret meetings. Among the other Americans who turned up for the 1974 command-performance were NATO Commander-General Andrew Goodpaster, George Ball, David Rockefeller, and the good Democratic Senator from the State of Minnesota, Walter F. Mondale. (5).

Add to all these grim facts the reality that many of these same conspirators control the purse strings of almost each and every major foundation, and know that they use this control to channel billions of dollars into the international socialist and communist schemes of world domination. American and Western European funds and foundation-monies have financed every act of population enslavement ever since the one-worlder's first sent Lenin and Trotsky back into Russia, long after the battles had been fought and won by the non-communist forces who had tired of the Czar's oppression and tyranny. Once back in Russia, they (Lenin and Trotsky) gained, by subtrafuge and duplicity, the needed control of the disorganized and struggling forces trying to form a new government. These same forces financed Mao back out

27

of the mountains of China, where the nationalist forces had driven him and his rag-tag band of Moscow-inspired revolutionaries. More recently they financed the Castro regime, on other recorded occasions they have worked behind the scenes with such unlikely spokesmen as Smuts, Stresemann, and Gandhi. They are the doctrinaire and financial pillar behind every important socialist and communist-front organization now active here in our land, as they slowly eat away at the very fabric of our life style.

How many of us realize that many foundations and funds, such as the Institute for Pacific Relations and its American council, are all interlocked to the Morgan, Astor, Carnegie, and Rockefeller fortunes? And that these fortunes are all *very* closely allied to such Wall Street firms as Standard Oil (one of the prime movers in the recently fabricated energy crisis, which was calculated to and does bleed many more billions of dollars from the long-suffering American motorist), I.T.T. (revealed as the lurking influence behind the attempt to buy the city of San Diego for Richard Nixon and the Republican convention), G.E., and the Chase National and National City Banks of New York (both revealed as opening branches in Moscow during this period of detente). That is most certainly an impressive lineup of capitalistic giants, who both this book and others before now, have uncovered and pin-pointed as the benefactors and the financial godfathers of international socialism and collectivism.

While you are thinking about those disturbing facts, add this one. There is an almost total subservience to the collectivist ideology of the leadership of the ivy-league universities, along with the seats of learning at Chicago, and California (including Stanford). Perhaps this helps you understand the almost complete stranglehold these conspirators have stealthily developed over American finance, indusry, education, and government. The Nixon play (which was sold to the American public as a great diplomatic accomplishment) of detente with the Soviets was probably planned many years ago, by the international monopolists, knowing full well that the two major forces would have to kiss and make up before an effective one-world partnership could be formed. The seemingly surprising warmup recently to Red China really began soon after the Second World War, when the international monopolists very effectively withdrew support from the Chaing Kai-shek regime, which in effect supported Mao's march from the mountains. For the full and true tale of this classic sell-out of a former ally, I recommend reading General Albert C. Wedemeyer's book about those now-historic events (6).

The good general was the last American commander in China during the Second World War. The book reveals that General George C. Marshall, the infamous architect of the immense monetary give-away called the "Marshall Plan," was the internationalist's hatchet-man. Understanding this, the current roles of Nixon, Kissinger, Ford, and Rockefeller are far more clear. They are simply acting out the roles assigned them by the Round Table (Bilderberg Group) powers, as their part in the continuing struggle for future world domination.

To stress this control point, consider if you will, two seemingly unrelated world-wide incidents of recent times, as I continue to show how advanced the plot is, and how we, the American public, have been programmed to underestimate the consequences. Incident number one took place in Asia. When the Pakistan-Bangladesh fighting was finished, the popularly acclaimed leader of the newly formed nation of Bangladesh did not do what would be considered quite the normal thing in such circumstances. He did not rush home to the cheers of his people and then assume his leadership role. His very first action was to rush off to London (the birthplace and seat of the Round Table) to confer with certain leaders in that city for the next forty-eight (48) hours. That seems strange behavior for the leader of a supposedly independent country. As the great unwashed millions awaited his triumphant return to his newly independent homeland, this leader was being schooled in the hallowed halls of London what his next moves should be, and when. Finally — two days after liberation — the leader returned, home at last to the cheers of the awaiting millions.

Incident number two happened half way across the world in the Mediterranean area. During a recent upheaval, when the leader of Cypress was forcefully removed from his position by a military coup, instead of that leader rushing to the so-called world court and forum, the United Nations, to plead his case, he rushed to London. Doesn't it seem just a bit odd that London, with an apparent lack of world strength militarily, should be so popular with leaders from around the world, in times of trouble? The Cypress leader then stayed in London for several days for a full round of top-secret talks. Could he have been conferring with the real leaders of his land? Then, as sort of an ironic icing on the political cake, Nixon dispatched his top aide, Joseph Sisco (see the membership list of the C.F.R. at the end of the chapter), to London to be briefed and to present the U.S. position about the Cypress situation. You say that sounds quite normal for the U.S. to be concerned about a NATO ally and to send an envoy to find out what was really happening from the horses mouth. Certainly, save for the fact that while Sisco was winging his way to London to discuss the problem, the Cypress leader was then winging his way to the U.S. to address the U.N.

The zinger comes when one realizes that both travel itineraries were well publicized well in advance to either parties boarding the planes for their respective trips. In other words, Mr. Sisco was going to London to confer with the same people with whom the deposed leader had just finished conferring with — the group of internationalists who control the moves of both and who seek to control you in the same manner. Joseph Sisco was not interested in meeting with the Cypriot, he was to meet with the real powers behind the scenes and they remained in London when the former leader came to New York to plead his case. Do you think that Bangladesh and Cyprus and their connections with London was coincidence? If so, the internationalists propaganda has been successful.

So, I have pinpointed the sources of many of our contemporary financial and political woes in this chapter, starting with Ruskin and following, in a very surface manner, some of the others, to the present day conspirators and their co-conspirators. I am sorry that it has to be presented in such a shallow, surface manner, but to attempt to go into any depth would require a very thick book to deal with the political agents and the deceit of the Round Table/Bilderberg Group alone. To attempt to put in writing all of the financial arms these people control would require a set of tomes the size of a good set of encyclopedias.

Prince Bernhard and Henry Kissinger and all of their present day fellow-plotters are knowingly leading us down the primrose path to national oblivion and personal slavery. They are saying one thing and acting in an opposite manner. They are very dangerous.

Prince Bernhard of the Royal Dutch Shell Oil Company and David Rockefeller of Standard Oil are but two members of the exposed "Bilderberg Group," As previously explained, Bilderberg is the contemporary name for the inner-circle conspirators of the Round Table clique. Here are a few more members who are now known. Public figures like Lester Pearson (former Canadian Prime Minister), Pierre-Paul Scheitzer (Director of the U.N.'s International Monetary Fund), Dirk Stikker (Secretary General of NATO), Gardner Cowles (publisher of Look magazine), J. William Fulbright (former Senator from Arkansas who, after many years of serving the cause of one-world-ism in the Senate, has been put out to pasture by an awakening electorate in his home state, and whose scholarships — the Fulbright scholars — are dedicated to the same subversive goals as the Rhodes scholars, which they were patterned after), Jacob Javits (another Senator whose main area of concern is geographically not a part of the United States, but rather the near and middle east), H. J. Heinz II (the president of Heinz Foods), David McDonald (the president of the United Steelworkers Union), and Cyrus Eaton (the multi-millionaire industrialist who has long advocated a union between the U.S.A. and the U.S.S.R.).

The listings of names and groups could go on and on,

it seems. We are being sold out from every possible side and position and by many persons of great influence and wealth. The danger is both emminent and real. The only roadblock to having an American President attend an international conference of socialist governments, like the recent one held during the summer in 1974 in London, England, is the masses of grass-roots American citizens. Such conferences are constantly held, but we in America hear very little concerning them, because we just might start putting two and two together and coming up with four. The only reason that any mention of this conference seeped into the controlled American press (guess who controls it), is the fact that the security forces had to be beefed-up tremendously at Heathrow Airport in London. when the Israeli Prime Minister was due to arrive, because of the threat of Arab terrorist actions.

You would generally think of such countries as England, Sweden and Israel as freedom-loving democratic republics. Yet they, and many more so-called Western nations have socialistic forms of government; and please keep in mind the statement that I made early in this book: To the conspirators socialism and communism are but two sides of a single coin. They are philosophies with a common goal. It's simply a matter of semantics.

You and I, the silent majority, Mr. and Mrs. Middle America, are the only bulwark in the path of these plotters. In a very real sense this makes us, you and I, the only remaining hope for the entire world, since communism and socialism has already taken its deadly toll in so many other "free" lands. The countdown to depression we now endure and suffer, and it will be the largest depression ever suffered by an industrialized nation, is just another stage on the part of the one-world international monopolists to demoralize and to confuse the American public. It is designed to ease the planned take-over. We must fully comprehend this to understand the domination of rampant crime in the streets of all of our major metropolitan areas, the smile-and wink-corruption of many of our elected officials from the very top to the local levels of the governmental structure, the dizzying

Prince Bernhard of the Netherlands, head of the secret, one world Bilderberger movement, confers with President Nixon. A former Nazi SS storm trooper ("We had a lot of fun"), Bernhard now works with the Rothschilds and Communists to promote a World Super State of the elite. Bernhard holds yearly secret meetings with high U. S. officials, bankers and industrialists to map plans for merging the U. S. and the Soviet Union into a world government.

Edmond and Guy de Rothschild, leaders of the French Rothschild clan. The Rothschilds are closely connected with Prince Bernhard in business (Royal Dutch Shell) and in the building of a one world super-government with the Soviets. Time of Dec. 20, 1963, says of Guy: "Guy is every inch a Rothschild. He personifies much of what the family name stands for . . . He is a friend and confidante of some of France's politicians . . . Most of all, he is dedicated to enlarging the fortune of his bank . . . Guy heads a versatile clan of modern day Rothschilds." Edmond, reputedly the richest of the French Rothschilds, is worth $500 million personally, according to estimates.

heights of inflation, the many strikes which plague our industry (7),, a general lack of quality in the products we purchase, and the shameful starvation of our golden-agers and inner-city officials, in the heart of this land of plenty.

There follows a partial list of members and former members of the Council on Foreign Relations: George Louis Beer, Walter Lippmann, Frank Aydelotte, Whitney Shepardson, Thomas W. Lamont, Jerome D. Greene, Edward D. Canham, Philip Kerr, J. P. Morgan, John W. Davis, Paul Cravath, Owen D. Young, Russell C. Leffingwell, Norman Davis, Allen Dulles, Geo. W. Wickersham, Frank L. Polk, Isaiah Bowman, Stephan P. Duggan, Otto Kahn, Willard Straight, Payne Whitney, Jock Whitney, Cornelius Vanderbilt Whitney, Michael Whitney Straight, Nicholas Murray Butler, Thomas N. Perkins, Charles Seymour, Elihu Root, Arthur H. Dean, Philip D. Reed, John J. McCloy, Abraham Flexner, Lewis Douglas, Douglas Dillon, Jacob Schiff, Felix and Paul Warburg, Dwight Marrow, Grayson Murphy, George Peabody, Henry P. Davidson, Corliss Lamont, Frederick Vanderbilt Field, Owen Lattimore, Joseph P. Chamberlain, Philip Jessup, William Lockwood, John K. Fairbanks, Dean Rusk, Alger Hiss, John Foster Dulles, James T. Shotwell, Christian Herter, Harold Stassen, Nelson Rockefeller (a single heart-beat away from the presidency?), Dean Acheson, Henry Cabot Lodge, Charles Yost, Arthur Burns, Harlan Cleveland, George Ball, Robert Murphy, Walter and Victor Reuther, Richard P. Peterson, Alan Pifer, Dr. Paul McCracken, Ellsworth Bunker, Gen. A. J. Goodpaster, Dr. Glenn T. Seaborg, Joseph Sisco (among other things, the recent Cypress courier), Jacob Beam, Gerald Smith, Paul Hoffman, Robert Hutchins (of University and think-tank fame), Mc George Bundy, and last but not least Henry Kissinger.

Believe it or not that is a much abbreviated list of just some of the more noted members that it would be easy for you to find in the "Who's Who." If I were to try to make just a list of all of the current members who are loyal to the C.F.R., along with the co-conspirators in international secret organizations dedicated to making America a part of the one-world control, the size of this book would easily double.

(1) *Rustin Today* by Kenneth Clark — Holt, Rinehart and Winston, 1964

(2) *Time Magazine,* 15 July, 1974

(3) *None Dare Call It Conspiracy* by Gary Allen with Larry Abraham, Concord Press, P.O. Box 2686, Seal Beach, Calif. 90740 — 1971

(4) Ibid.

(5) *Las Vegas Review-Journal,* in an article written by A.P. writer John Gale, Monday, July 1, 1974, page #24

(6) *Wedemeyer Reports* by General Albert C. Wedemeyer — Henry Holt Co. 1958

(7) "Run-away Inflation Triggers Most Strikes Since Lats 40's," headline in the L.V. Review-Journal, Tuesday, July 16, 1974

Chapter Three

THE CASE HISTORY of the SELL-OUT

After the presidential power incursion on private lives during the Civil War and the resulting loss of private banking rights to a federally-controlled banking system, the United States' financial fortunes resembled the flights of fancy on an amusement park roller-coaster. Up we went with the inflations, down we tumbled with the recessions and the depressions. By the latter part of the nineteenth century the pace of federal intervention had accelerated. This interference culminated with the passage of the Income Tax Amendment and the Federal Reserve Act in 1913.

With these two laws on the books, the early one-worlders were now ready to hasten our American path towards socialism. We were pretty well established as a nation of isolationists, except for the protection of international American lives and property (as shown in the cases of the Barbary Coast pirate period or during the Rough Rider saga in Cuba). In order to further involve America in the affairs of the world, we were duped into a series of events which led to our eventual entry as a combatant in the European War, which has since been misnamed by the internationalist-historians as the First World War. (1).

It was most necessary to involve the U.S. in the European power struggles, in order to make easier the propagandizing the American public into the one-world way of thought. Like so many of our recent Presidents, Woodrow Wilson was elected by the American public on his firm promise to keep America out of European politics, affairs and wars. His campaign slogan was "He Kept Us Out of War!" Like just as many Presidents, once in office, Wilson allowed the reality to become just the opposite of the many campaign promises and pledges that he had made. He acted in a manner directly counter to the mandate of the peoples will. As a result of the sophisticated propaganda barrage, very soon thereafter an aroused American army of doughboys went "over there" with an instilled sense of dedication and vengeance and "helped save the world."

What really happened, rhetoric aside, is that America squandered a great many of its most vital possessions, the lives of the young, on the bloody battlefields flung across Europe and ended up becoming hopelessly entangled in the political and the financial intrigues of the continent. One 'Colonel' Edward Mandell House, an English financier, was the main power influencing President Woodrow Wilson during this time and it was he (House) who was responsible for many of the one-world steps that were taken by our nation during that period of time. 'Colonel' House was supported and backed-up in all these socialistic actions by the Schiffs, the Warburgs, the Kahns, the Rockefellers, and the Morgans — the big-money powers of the times. In plain and simple language, 'Colonel' House was the intriguing financial "establishments" inside man at the White House.

It is interesting to note, at this point, that from those humble non-isolationist beginnings, just after the turn of the century, when our involvement in others affairs was at an absolute minimum, and a national debt was practically unknown, that we are now in all nations internal affairs and we are now struggling under a national indebtedness that will probably round out somewhere around the ridiculous figure of Five-hundred *billion* dollars in 1974. It boogles the mind to realize that just the interest on this tremendous sum alone is more than thirty *billion* dollars annually.

As a people, we tend to become jaded because of our familiarity with certain terms and amounts which we read and hear almost daily in the news. But let me remind you that a *million* dollars is a great deal of money. A *billion* dollars is a *thousand* times the amount of a million, and I am stating that because of wars and our international position of supporting most of the rest of the world financially, we now have a five-hundred *billion* dollar national debt. If it were not for the financing of death-dealing war products and our vain attempts to buy friendships and loyalty around the world, I wonder how many hungry people we could feed right here in our own back yard and how many sick people we could nurse back to productive health, with just a small portion of that huge amount of money? How many senior ciizens could stop supplementing their inflationary-crippled diets with pet food and other sub-human survival tactics, if we could divert part of the money we now waste in subsidizing food programs and industrial machinery exports for our avowed enemies, to the benefit of elderly people, allowing them to live out their final years in dignity and peace?

The not-so-funny joker in the deck is the fact that these selfsame 'Colonel' House backers (the Schiffs, the Warburgs, the Kahns, the Rockefellers, and the Morgans), their heirs, and their co-conspiratorial international monopolists, now greedily collect this vast thirty-billion dollar interest bonanza (2), caused by the federal debt, which was really caused by their influence in the first place. Think about that, if you will. The same people, by and large, who caused us to begin our current trend to financial oblivion on the federal level, through their one-world plotting and other intrigues, are the self-same interests who now reap the huge wind-fall profits which result from the interest which must be paid on these national debts.

The one-worlder's hand-picked representatives and flunkies are always placed in key and strategic positions within the framework and bureaucracy of the U.S. Federal Reserve System. This is precisely where the national-debt loans are negotiated and the thirty-*billion* dollar gift-bonanza placement is determined. Placement is the key word. This strategy is what the plotters call pressure from the top, pressure from the bottom. I will more fully explore this tactic in the socialistic/communistic never-ending-pressures campaign in a later chapter.

The man who pioneered the idea of the central bank

J. P. Morgan created artificial panic used as excuse to pass Federal Reserve Act. Morgan was instrumental in pushing U. S. into WWI to protect his loans to British government. He financed Socialist groups to create an all-powerful centralized government which international bankers would control at the apex from behind the scenes. After his death, his partners helped finance the Bolshevik Revolution in Russia.

German born international financier P a u l Warburg masterminded - establishment of Federal Reserve to put control over nation's economy in hands of international bankers. The Federal Reserve controls the money supply which allows manipulators to create alternate cycles of boom and bust, i.e., a roller coaster economy. This allows those in the know to make fabulous amounts of money, but even more important, allows the Insiders to control the economy and further centralize power in the federal government.

of the United States (the Federal Reserve System) was a German immigrant by the name of Paul Warburg (check your CFR list again). Of historical importance is the fact that Paul Warburg had a brother who remained behind in Germany and who later became a major money source for the Russian revolution. Paul Warburg married into the big-money American/international banking firm of Kuhn, Loeb, and Company. A third brother, fellow immigrant Felix Warburg, married the daughter of Jacob Schiff, the powerful American financier and member of the international big-money cartel. Further in regards to that particular family name is the fact that the Schiffs and the Rothschilds once shared a double-house in Frankfurt, Germany, a few centuries before the time we are now taking a look at. No revelation of any international financial intrigue or control is even seemingly complete without the inclusion somewhere of the name Rothschild. If a single family name and financial source could be traced to all of the one-worlders intrigues, it most certainly would be the name Rothschild.

So complete is the financial dynasty of Mayer Amschel Rothschild (1743-1812), that no capital transaction of consequence can be negotiated to this very day, without having at least the shadow of the House of Rothschild affect the outcome in some manner. Mayer Rothschild started out in life to become a Rabbi. He ended up dominating the entire world financially. Somewhere along the way Mayer Rothschild found that his talents were more given to the earthly matters of economics, than to spiritual matters. He established and successfully ruled the German Central Bank. His sons were each sent out with a mission and they all founded equally successful banks throughout Europe.

The eldest son, Amschel, remained in Germany to help his father and eventually to inherit control of the German bank. Solomon, the next son, founded the Vienna Bank and became an all-powerful figure in the Austro-Hungarian Empire. The third son, Nathan, then established the bank in London, where he went to become the most powerful figure in that kingdom. Carl, the fourth son did much the same thing in Italy, and Jacob (also known as James), the youngest Rothschild, dominated the destiny of France through the bank that he founded in Paris. All of these above facts are now history and are easily researched for validity. And please be advised that the Rothschilds and their heirs are still the dominant figures controlling international economies until this very day and hour. You don't read the Rothschild name in the press as frequently as you read about the Goulds, the Kennedys, the Fords, or the Rockefellers, but believe me, their blood is well represented in the councils of the rich and the powerful.

There was an article in some papers at the end of last year (1973) which told of the activities of the sixty-year old Baroness Batsheva de Rothschild, the " . . . first member of the Jewish banking dynasty to make her home in the promised land (Israel). For nearly a dozen years she has lived in a beautifully landscaped modern home just outside Tel Aviv, quietly dispensing her own fortune to support arts and crafts, science, music, and the dance in Israel. She grew up in luxury . . ." The article went on to say that the Baroness' great-uncle, Baron Edmond Rothschild, began financing Jewish colonization of Palestine in the 1880's. Her father Edouard de Rothschild headed the French branch of the family. Her cousin, the present Baron Edmond de Rothschild, runs the empire his grandfather built and is currently constructing a luxury golf resort at Caesarea, near where the Romans threw Jesus to the lions a few centuries past. Her brother, Baron Guy de Rothschild now heads the French banking house and is the president of the United Jewish Appeal in France. Her cousins are the leading fund raisers for Israel in Britain. (3).

That article was the exception to the rule, the rule is that they shun publicity and prefer to operate unknown by the general public at large, known only by business associates and rich intimates. Every once in a great while a small, discreet news articles about a Rothschild wedding may appear in print, but seldom any more than that type of token mention is made of them in print.

41

I recall a few years ago that a New York-based Rothschild fooled around with the "pretty-people" play-boying it and ended up being garroted with a silk stocking about his neck, when found in his ultra-plush New York City penthouse. After a few sensational-type stories, a Rothschild-imposed blackout on the news regarding his untimely demise was enforced and little was ever again seen in print about the affair.

So through the efforts of the Rothschilds, the Warburgs, and the mysterious 'Colonel' House, America was reluctantly becoming a part of world-wide economics and politics. You will recall that I mentioned that both the Rothschilds and Warburgs came from Germany. 'Colonel' House was a native of England. This meant that our national destiny was being guided by a consortium of foreigners, with obvious foreign interests replacing our *national* best interests. In the 1912 Presidential elections, both Woodrow Wilson and Teddy Roosevelt solemnly denounced Wall Street. In truth, both these men were representatives and agents for Wall Street and the international monopolist interests. The one-worlders deceived us. Heads they win; tails we lose. The deck was stacked and we joined the crooked game in good faith, without the slightest chance to win.

It is much like our present-day political parties and the candidates, each out promising the other on their plans to cut the federal budget. Once they win the elections and settle into office, both of them go on an orgy of spending that makes the preceeding administration seem conservative by comparison. It is time that an aroused citizenry put all of these oil-toungued orators out of office.

Joining the Warburgs and the other shadowy manipulators around this difficult period of time in our history (1910-1930) was Bernard Baruch. Baruch is oftimes eulogized as the financial advisor to five or six American Presidents. Perhaps a more realistic description would be to refer to him as the employer of the five or six. I will return to the tricks of Mr. Baruch in a little while.

If you are now asking, what do all of these facts mean

to me? One simple answer is that the interest on our national debt is itself the third largest item in the federal budget. Who do you think labors long and hard to pay off that interest? That's right, you and I! It means that our withering gold reserves have been mortgaged to foreign interests and that most of our silver has long since left these shores.

Silver and gold are the only real international forms of monies and without them, as a nation, we are broke. Our stockpiles and reserves of silver and gold are gone only because of the chicanery and the deception of the ruling clique of international bankers. They planned it and willed it so, in order to help weaken us, as a people, for their planned takeover.

At the time of the Luistana incident, we were being led like gentle, trusting lambs to the slaughter-alters of one-world big money by a variety of Judas goats. The Lusitania was carrying six million pounds of J. P. Morgan-financed munitions to England and the ship itself was a British Naval auxiliary cruiser. That is a warship no matter how you look at it and they knew it. The passengers had been amply warned by a series of full page newspaper ads explaining the ship's role in the increasing European conflict. There were even German-American pickets at the landing ramps of the New York docks, reminding the passengers that they were taking a luxury cruise on a warship, and that venture was risky, at best. Despite all the warnings, the passengers embarked and the Lusitania was indeed sunk. As a result, America became involved in the very war that President Wilson promised to keep us out of only a short time before. Bernard Baruch was made a virtual dictator of American business, when President Wilson appointed him the Chairman of the War Industries Board. It is widely held that Mr. Baruch made himself a neat two-hundred million dollars as a direct result of that appointment and the war. Not adverse to turning a quick profit as a result of human and American suffering, it is said that Mr. Baruch made many millions more by cornering the silver market as a result of his insider-privy information, just before the big crash in 1929. So these are a few insights into one of our so-called dedicated public servants, a respected financial advisor and elder statesman, now deceased, who amassed several great fortunes out of several national misfortunes. I feel very strongly that he and all of those like him, who profit from our patriotism and who are dedicated to the one-world designs on our freedoms, need to be unmasked, as I have just done, before the court of public opinion, as the schemers and the agents of outside interests which our research and study has shown them to be.

It was the U.S. intervention in the First World War that helped make possible the collapse of imperialist Russia and to the eventual takeover of that nation by the agents of international communism. Pages 66 through 72 of "None Dare Call It Conspiracy" by Gary Allen will take the interested reader step by step through that infamous turning point in world history. Rest assured, no matter which controlled version of world history you may have read, it was anything *but* the masses of Russians who put the communists in control of Russia. It has only been the ruthless and determined suppression against the will of the Russian masses which has been able to retain power for the gang in charge of the Kremlin in the years since that takeover. The book "Conspiracy" will tell you the inside story of some of the strange angels who supplied the gold for Lenin and his well-heeled return to Russia after the revolution. Some equally odd American backers were supplying Trotsky and his cohorts with all the cash they needed in their bid for power. When the news accidently reached the American press about the key role in financing played by Max Warburg in the Russian revolutionary plot, his naturalized-American brother Paul was quietly forced to resign from his key post, in our country, as the head of our Federal Reserve System. The other naturalized-American brother, Felix, had a father-in-law who was the chief bank-teller of the Trotsky-factio of the international communist movement out of New York City, in their abortive bid to take control

44

of the then reeling post-revolutionary government in Russia.

I have now very briefly outlined the total involvement of the international monopolists and their American cohorts, in our unnecessary inclusion in the European War and their simultaneous financing of the communist/socialist conspiracy during the days of the Russian power upheaval. I have tried to show you that the name of the game is power, that the trump cards are international economics and the rules are conceived and devised by these same financial manipulators world-wide.

I am uncovering some of these manipulators for your benefit. Forewarned is forearmed. Make no mistake about the protagonists nor the stakes involved. These roles and goals are cut and dried. They are as clean as black and white. On the one hand, we have our individual freedoms and our capitalistic choices in our existing democratic Republic, and on the other hand we have the iron fist of dictatorial powers and police states, and the limited choices available under scientific socialism and totalitarian communism. You and I are in this deadly serious game and the stakes are freedom versus slavery, with the winner taking all ! !

(1) *"The Lusitania"* by Colin Simpson
(2) *"The Naked Capitalist"* by W. Clean Skousen — The Reviewer, 2197 Berkeley St., Salt Lake City, Utah 84109
(3) Article from AP (Tel Aviv) in L.V. Review-Journal, 13, Dec. 1973

Chapter Four

CASE HISTORIES OF
U.S. INTERNATIONALISM

Woodrow Wilson and the League of Nations was the earliest full scale attempt on the part of the monetary barons to bring the United States into the political and financial intrigues of Europe on a continuing scale. In fact, by the time of the establishment of the League of Nations, it had been clearly shown that we were the only real obstacle to the institution of the pioneer one-worlders (ala Plato, Ruskin, and Rhodes). The power-and-money-brokers in Europe had clearly shown that military power and subtrefuge could easily accomplish their goals on all the other continents. They rushed armies and missionaries all across Asia and Africa, seizing huge chunks of territory under a dozen different guises. At the Berlin conferences at the end of the nineteenth century, Africa was systematically paralled out to the European participants to the meet. Armed conquest raced across the valleys and highlands of Asia. Miniscule monarchies became world powers because of their colonial holdings (example Portugal). But here, directly in the path of this mad rush for power and control of the world's resources, stood America. America — young, strong, and brave, and unwilling to bow to any outside power and pressure. America, the only bulwark in the plan for total global domination by the lusters-after-power. We were too strong for them to challenge us face to face, so what they were unable to accomplish through their armed power, they decided to attempt through the ploy of deceit.

The League of Nations was the first serious and concerted effort to involve America in and to finally make America a part of their world government. Woodrow Wilson was a leading architect of and vocal proponent for our (America) helping to found this proposed early world watchdog supergovernment. It is often said that the best laid plans of mice and men often go awry. Somewhere between the plans and the planners, something went awry and America did not fall for the scheme. They (the plotters) felt that with President Wilson so strongly involved in the formation of the League of Nations, that America was a sure bet to participate. Allow me to use a humorous simile in order to state what really happened: The poisoned plate was carefully prepared and set in place for the proposed guest of honor and *victim;* and guess who didn't come to dinner?

This League of Nations farce was a classic example of the frustrations suffered by the international intriguers when their well-laid plots failed to achieve their desired goals by fate and chance. During the League of Nations era, few, if any, observers on the national and international scene could have guessed that some power-hungry schemers in far-away Germany, France, Italy, and England, were carefully planning the demise of our democratic form of government. They plotted so that they could eventually control and rule our country as they were doing in so many countries at that time. Keep in mind that this was all happening even *before* the communist takeover in Russia and the much-later establishment of the fact that the new rulers of this form of government *also* had some very strong designs on world conquest and world control.

It is exactly this fact which brings to the surface one of the most interesting facts that this book will uncover for your understanding: If these international monopolists and one-world financial plotters were active in the late years of the nineteenth century (the 1800's) and even more active in the earliest years of he twentieth century (the 1900's), how could they be the partners in crime of the international communist conspiracy? This disturbing revelation becomes crystal clear when we realize that the socialism/communism circle did not really assume any power until the second decade of the twentieth century, and did not become a real world power until the fourth and fifth decades of this century. In other words, the communist power was pre-dated by the one-world monopolists designs for world power by from thirty to sixty years.

Putting that sequence of events into its correct historical perspective and then remembering that Cecil Rhodes' establishment of the super-secret Round Table Group occurred in 1891, then it begins to make sense that the Round Table plot to rule the world clearly is older than the communist plot to do the same. The next logical conclusion is that either the big-money manipulators are using the communists for their own purposes, or that vica versa is the truth.

Since the big-money boys started their drive for world domination first and since they have also subsidized all of the subsequent communist take-overs on a world-wide basis, it is fairly logical to assume that the one-world international monopolists see the potential to achieve their goals via the route of communist-supported causes and through the covert financial aid for communist revolutions where ever they may occur.

It is also logical to assume that since the big-money boys are mainly drawn from the rich elite, they reason that the masses will not trust their cause, but that the communist rhetoric about workers paradises and share and share alike programs for the masses has just such an appeal. In other words the communists offer the financial manipulators the key to public support for their cause.

It is also fair to assume that these financial manipulators do not support these totalitarian forms of government in hopes of becoming just another part of the common masses when all of the plotting is finished and their goals have been accomplished. The money manipulators have a deep-seated motivation to rule the world. Through clandestine connections they have everything that they need to accomplish this goal, everything but the man-power needed to populate an enforcement arm necessary to insure this role. The socialists/communists camp came along and seemed to have the emotional and idealogical appeal needed to make inroads into the minds of the masses. They had perfected the verbalized utopian talk

48

about the share and share alike doctrines, which have great appeal to the have-nots. But the socialist/communist camp, for all of this mass appeal, had no financial base from which to launch their drive for power. So it was a marriage of convenience. The Round Table people had the money and the socialist/communists had the emotional appeal needed to garner the troops necessary for the perpetuation of the plan.

It has been said many times that politics make strange bedfellows. Never has that statement had more meaning than in the wedding of purpose between the capitalistic one-world power-hungry clique and the feverish converts to communistic doctrines. Every communist takeover since Lenin and Trotsky, on up through and including Chairman Mao and Island dictator Castro, has been backed and achieved with Round Table-sponsored money. Keep in mind that the current name for these international plotters is the Bilderberg Group, under the leadership of Prince Bernhard of the Netherlands, and that they command most world leaders, including the Americans, to attend their super-secret meetings at their will and whim. Remember also that the Council on Foreign Relations is directly under their control, and that it greatly influences America's foreign policy.

The obvious aim for the money-monopolists is to allow the socialist/communists to achieve power on a world-wide basis. Once this is accomplished, the big-money brokers feel that they will then be able to assume the mantle of leadership, by what-ever-means-necessary, and take over this supra-world-government from their communist lackeys. They know that they can now count on their inclusion in the world-wide ruling consortium, since they have been patient partners-in-crime with the communist conspiracy from the beginning.

What they want is control and the disciplined armies of the commies can deliver this desire to them. They then plan to use these control armies to insure world peace (who would they fight, if they ruled all?) and to insure peak world production to further fill their money coffers. That is the final simple key to the entire plot,

49

the control of peak world production power. Do you realize what it would mean to own and to control everything in the entire world? They do!!!

If they achieve their goals, these money-mad, power-seekers will grow rich and powerful beyond their wildest dreams. They cloak their schemes for control within such lofty-sounding catch-phrases as, "A world devoid of crime and wars," or, "A peaceful earth where hunger and poverty are unknown." Don't fall under their spell, don't be lulled by such simplistic slogans, for these people are really talking about a ruthless and dictatorial regime which kills or imprisons any opposition to its will and allows the living only minimal slave-like conditions of existence. They want to take away all of our freedom and have us serve their greed in silent subservience.

So the mysterious events of Rhodes' 1870 intrigues brought about the aborted attempt to ensnare us in the early one-world government scheme we now historically refer to as the League of Nations. Even when these initial attempts failed, these same tenacious forces continued their infiltration of the ruling institutions within our country. The attitudenal-acceptance schemes involving federal cooperative labor projects, under the leadership and guidance of one-worlder Franklin Delano Roosevelt, were next on their subversive agenda. The federally financed W.P.A., N.R.A., T.V.A., and the C.C.C. were the alphabetical titles for some of these new assaults on our system of private enterprise. Combining forces with the octopus-like ever-growing, civil service, rank-and-file network of federal jobs, the Roosevelt era mass make-work projects and public testing of acceptance of other ideas provided models and valuable insights as to just what directions the one-worlder's would have to take in their next move to deprive us of our freedoms. For an example, the one-world marketing experts found that the make-work projects, like the W.P.A., etc, garnered no loyalty nor espirit-de-corps from the participants in such projects. They established that the recruits mainly served their time and then took their newly acquired skills out into the private sector of business and industry, whenever and wherever possible.

If the one-worlders have an ultimate forte, that talent would have to be their patience and their tenacity. They know well how to bide their time. Their next overt move was in 1939 when the American-based Council on Foreign Relations set up a Committee of Post-War Problems. This move is especially interesting when you consider that this committee was established a full two years before the United States became involved in the second European land war, once again misnamed a World War. We would have understood the committee if we had understood that the one-world plotters had long since made the necessary preparations for our inclusion in that holocaust. This committee, as I stated, was a part of the Council on Foreign Relations, and it (the committee) was the forerunner of several other efforts, like the Dumbarton Oaks Conference (1), which eventually led to the establishment of the one-worlders second grandiose attempt at a global government by deceit, the well-known United Nations plan.

The United Nations was founded in San Francisco, California during the year of 1945 (so be on the lookout for some mighty propaganda barrages telling us how lucky we have been to subsidize this world supra-government on the occasion of the upcoming thirteenth anniversary in the fall of 1975). Among the American delegates to this founding of a proposed one-world super-global-state were: Harold Stassen, Owen Lattimore, Philip Jessup, Nelson Rockefeller, Harry Dexter White, John Foster Dulles, Alger Hiss, Dean Acheson, and John Carter Vincent. That's quite a collection of convicted traitors and spies intermingled with many of our top elected and appointed officials, by any standard. All of that above list and thirty-eight other American delegates were all members in good standing of the Council on Foreign Relations, which, like the name of Rothschild, seems to forever be where people plot and scheme to take our freedoms away. Of course these delegates and their supporters will agrue that it is merely coincidental that this motley assortment of traitors, in league with high U.S. officials, ended up founding what is the latest attempt at the consolidation of world power. It is also obvious that they have been vastly more successful this time. I think that it is more than mere concidence.

It is interesting to take note of the tenacious reach for prestige and power by the Rockefeller group. This is especially true in light of the recent developments on the national scene and the added prominence which has been attached to the post of vice president. From scion of one of the robber-baron families, to one of the founding fathers of the one-worlders United Nations, to the appointed post of Vice President, is all a part of this tenacity on the part of Nelson Rockefeller.

The well-known liberal stance of Nelson Rockefeller was of no real concern to the supposedly conservative stance as espoused by the appointed President, Gerald R. Ford, during his deliberations to select a Vice President. The reason for this willingness on the part of both parties to overlook the supposed and obvious past differences, is the now-evident fact that there are no real deviations in either one's mind about the direction of federal policies and practices. They both are representatives of the same group of financial politicians (finpolitans) who deal in the shadowy international world of financial control and socialistic political reality.

As these international financial despots pull the strings behind the scenes to move our government ever closer to their one - world dreams of total control, the so - called idealogical schisms are narrowed visably, to give the public the illusion of a new, liberal/conservative national unity and rededicated sense of purpose, which seemingly transcends the usual considerations of partisan politics.

Actually, what is really happening, is that the entire scenario is being acted out by all the principals, in an extension of the continual testing of the general public's acceptance of a total-one-party system. If this premise is accepted within the divided Republican party, the next step will probably be a short period of unheard-of-nonpartisan cooperation between the two main national

Nelson Rockefeller and Richard Nixon are theoretically political enemies, but Rocky arranged '68 election so that if he could not be President, someone whom he controlled would be. The Rockefeller family, through their Chase Manhattan Bank and other entities, have been great benefactors of the Soviet Union ever since Communist Revolution in Russia. During campaign Nixon promised to halt shipment of war materials from America to North Vietnam via European Communist bloc because these supplies were being used to kill American soldiers. But much of this bloc trade is controlled by Rockefellers and Nixon has reversed himself and greatly multiplied such trade. The press, quite naturally remained silent about killing American soldiers by proxy.

"Colonel" House (l) was front man for the international banking fraternity. He manipulated President Woodrow Wilson (r) like a puppet. Wilson called him "my alter ego." House played a major role in creating the Federal Reserve System, passing the graduated income tax and getting America into WWI. House's influence over Wilson is an example that in the world of super-politics the real rulers are not always the ones the public sees.

parties — the Democrats and the Republicans. After this staged experimental honeymoon in national politics, it is but a short step to then blend the two parties into a single ruling party, dominated of course, by the Council on Foreign Relations trained one-world agents. The final transition would be to the planned one-world international supra-government, with all of the big-brother features of the police/welfare state that this step would mean. The sooner that the plot is expedited, the sooner that these sinster forces would make their move to implement the plot to take away all of our liberty. The United States of America would then become just another colony to these finpolitans who lust for our liberty.

As a well aware, well-travelled, worldly American citizen, I find even the thought of that potential slavery on our hallowed shores, repulsive. I chose the word slavery with good reason, because, after all of the flowery talk and utopian promises, the outstanding truth about the one-world communism plot is, that it boils down to a singular fact. That fact is that it is now and always will continue to be a form of government which represents a life of repression, oppression, suppression and slavery for the masses, with the total authority being held by a very small and totally powerful inner-ruling clique. The rulers life and death words are law and there is no court of appeal from their edicts and decisions.

It is of interest for this writer to go back to some very pointed and interesting observations made about the then-Governor of New York State, Nelson A. Rockefeller, by Ferdinand Lundberg, in his best selling 1968 book on the money powers that control America (2). The following excerpts are from that works:

"Although Vietnam is popularly accepted as an heroic dirt-level President's maximum effort, the operation has been formally and enthusiastically endorsed by Governor Nelson A. Rockefeller. It is, obviously, a venture carrying the highest finpolitan (3) sanction ... "

" . . . Professor Lipset as of 1960, thought it more

likely 'that Nelson A. Rockefeller, the liberal Republican Governor of New York, will ultimately prove to be a true representative of the revived pattern of direct participation in politics by members of the upper class' . . . "

"The Rockefeller Empire"

"The Rockefeller empire of contrapuntal profit and non-profit enterprises is here taken, purely for illustrative purposes, as the central and conventionally most creditable of such ostensible contribution, with allusion later to lesser similar finpolitan complexes. Currently this network is an international empire of industrial, financial, cultural, and political activities that for variety, quantity, and quality, put everything of a similar kind in the shade.

The present third generation of ruling Rockefellers—five sons and a daughter of John D., Jr., without considering the independent branch of the founder's brother, William — has at its fingertips what is the quintessence of many great fiefdoms, worthy to be included in a modern Arabian Nights tale. All of it is bone and muscle, none either of fat or meagerness. It is not only quantitatively but qualitatively rich, like a Christmas fruit-nut-brand cake.

The reigning Rockefeller brothers are: John D. the third (b. 1906), Nelson Aldrich (b. 1908), Laurence S. (b. 1910), Winthrop (b. 1912), and David (b. 1915). They have a sister, Mrs. Abby Mauze', who figures in the gilt-edge sextette, according to reports by family friends, pretty much as a silent partner. All appear to be of good intelligence, not the least of their assets, although actually the intelligence at their disposal — the pooled family intelligence deriving from long experience with a mercurical world plus that of their large professional advisory and research staff — greatly exceeds their personal intelligence. Like the ruler of a great state, they have far more relevant information at their ready disposition than they can carry with them in their own heads . . . "

" . . . The fourth, and even fifth, generations is being readied in the wings. At this writing there are more than twenty-three living members of the fourth generation . . . "

" . . . Some of these offspring are now married and themselves have children of the fifth Rockefeller generation, members of an established world dynasty (4) . . . "

So now we have to contend with twenty-nine years of entrenched power of the New York-based United Nations, right up the street, figuratively speaking, from their financial brokers on Wall Street, and their theoreticians residing in the stately halls of the Council on Foreign Relations, who it turns out, are interestingly housed right across the street in the Soviet U.N. mission headquarters. Need I point out the excellence of that infiltration of both our land and our largest major city?

Additionally, we have the powerful and subversive arms of the United Nations silently reaching into many other facets of American life, through their many social organizations and financial branches. A partial list of these groups would include UNICEF (a socialist dominated youth-oriented organization), The United Nations Emergency Relief Organization and fund (channeling millions in mostly American-sponsored dollars into those countries and areas who indicate a willingness to sing the socialist/communist songs of revolution — so to speak), the powerful and deadly International Monetary Fund, and the World Bank Organization.

Some of the other U.N. sponsored organizations are: UNESCO (the U.N. Educational, Scientific, and Cultural Organization), F.A.O. (the Food and Agricultural Organization), I.M.C.O. (Inter-governmental Maritime Consultive Organization), I.C.A.O. (International Civil Aviation Organization), I.L.O. (International Labor Organization), I.T.U. (International Telecommunications Union), U.P.U. (Universal Postal Union), W.H.O. (World Health Organization), and W.M.O. (World Meterological Organization). This list is but a partial unmasking of the United Nation's many arms into America's and into the world's affairs. Since this book deals primarily in the area of economics, I am now going to more closely examine two of the U.N. organizations: The World Bank and The International Monetary Fund.

(1) Dumbarton Oaks was an international conference held at a vast estate in Washington, D.C. from August until October 1944. There were 39 delegates in attendance from the U.S., England, Russia, and China.

(2) "The Rich and the Super-Rich" by Ferdinand Lundberg—Lyle Stuart, Inc., New York. Extensive quotes from pages 430, 3rd para., 566, 3rd para., 592, 3rd para., and 593, 1st, 2nd, and 3rd paragraphs.

(3) Finpolitan — is a Lundberg-coined word meaning financial politicians.

(4) Keep in mind that this appraisal was written in 1968, and that more members have been born into that dynasty, adding to the srength of the Rockefeller empire.

Chapter Five

THE INTERNATIONAL MONETARY FUND AND THE WORLD BANK

During the Kennedy and the Johnson administrations (1961-1968) Robert McNamara was one of the real powers to be reckoned with in Washington, D.C. Suddenly and without much forewarning, this powerful Secretary of Defense resigned his prestigious post and assumed the rather unheralded job as President of the World Bank. Many observers wondered alond at this switch in midstream by McNamara, to a post that at best seemed symbolic and non-functional. What most people could not have known (since only the real insiders could possibly know) was that the World Bank was on the very brink of assuming a real world role in finances and power. The international monopolists wanted to make sure that they had one of their own, equal to the task soon to be demanded, in the driver's seat of such an organization. Robert McNamara was such a man. Using the lessons he learned while he was President of the gigantic Ford Motor Company Empire, he has ruled the policies and fate of the World Bank with an iron fist ever since.

Robert Strange McNamara (1916-   ) Secretary of Defense 1961 to 1968. He was the *chief* advisor on economics and foreign affairs, in addition to functioning as the Secretary of Defense during both the Johnson and the Kennedy administrations. He was so powerful a figure that he shaped both our foreign policy as well as our economic directions during those years, while also filling his duties as the military chief of the nation. He initiated the method of military budget-projection which is still followed in the run-away Pentagon budgets in Washington today. Before being named Secretary of Defense, he taught at Harvard and was later the President of the Ford Motor Company. In 1968 McNamara resigned his government position to become the President of the International Bank for Reconstruction and Development. This U.N. organization is widely called the World Bank. The World Bank controls the following U.N. agencies: I.D.A. (the International Development Association) which lends money to governments on an easier basis than other agencies, I.F.C. (the International Finance Corporation), which lends money to private developments, and I.B.R.D. (the World Bank) which specializes in lending and controlling money granted for large governmental projects internationally.

The World Bank now controls the financial resources within the world's economy. The International Monetary Fund helps adjust the differences in the world's money systems, supposedly helping them to trade with each other with greater ease. Our fast-dwindling gold supply and our depleted silver reserve are but two of the dubious benefits that America has gained by being involved with these two U.N. organizations. Our once solid economy was used to bolster the sagging financial fortunes of both Western Europe and the Soviet Bloc after the Second World War. Using our money as collateral and for payments, foreign governments strengthened their economies at our expense. The simple secret to their seemingly healthy economic state today is that slave-labor costs next to nothing to sustain, and the work of the largely unenlightened work-forces elsewhere, costs but a little more. So their resources were gleaned and their production boomed on in unfair competition with our paid-workers and our industries. Our enemies were lean and hungry while we grew fat, complacent, and indolent.

Suddenly we were bombarded with west European cameras and other precision-type instruments that it cost a bundle to produce over here. There followed a flood of Asiaic-produced T.V.'s and a host of other audio paraphenalia. These imported products were being sold here in America for less than our rock bottom production costs amounted to. Then one day the bubble burst. We woke up to realize that we had supported and subsidized our own productive bankruptcy. Through the Marshall Plans and the hundreds of other 'be-munificient-to-your-former-foes' plans, we had at last managed to price many American-made products right out of the local and the international competitive marketplaces. At the other end of the spectrum, the American-based socialistic dominated labor unions kept on a constant pressure against manufacturers, industry, and other producers, for bigger and bigger employees paychecks. This is a classic exxample of the communist tactic of pressure from the top, pressure from the bottom, a tactic we will examine in greater detail a little later in the book.

Manufacturers were compelled by labor unions to pay even higher salaries to produce the same items which were flooding the American market at half the price the American-made items were forced to sell for. The Bridges and the Reuthers did their jobs well. It was a no-win situation for America and our hidden enemies well knew it. Adding insult to injury, it was the taxes from the same wage-earners and the hard-pressed manufacturers which subsidized (via the Marshall Plan and others) this unfair competition in the beginning. Perhaps you can now see how total, how vicious, and how cunning the plotting was by the one-worlders.

As a result of the cheap imports and the high costs of our native American production, we soon found that the "Balance of Payments" scale was out of kilter. The balance of payments are the total amount of goods brought into this country, less the total amount of goods sent out of this coutntry. If we send more out of the country than we take into the country, it indicates that somebody owes us some money. If, on the other hand, we take in more goods and produce than we send out, it means just the opposite — we owe somebody some money. This was the position in which we suddenly found ourselves.

A dozen or so years after we had won the Second World War, we found as a result of our informational and our monetary generosity, we were badly in debt to the very nations which we had defeated on earlier battlefields. (2) What the power-hungry clique could not achieve through the force of war, they seemed very well equipped to gain by subtrefuge during periods of peace. It has been shown that the World Bank is much more adept and efficient at that penetration of America than were all the massive Legions of Hitler or Hiroshito's suicide squads. Robert S. McNamara, with an assembly-line, precision knowledge, he no doubt gained administering the fortunes of Ford Motor Company, directed the strengthening of the entire socialistic world, at the expense of America.

The intrigue continues daily. Here is still another example that I'll bet most of working America missed. In a newstory datelined Washington, D.C., and appearing in the local press during the early summer months of 1974, the following story was carried. The headline read "You Will Never Own A SDR Or Even See One." This is part of the story that followed:

"Washington (AP)—There are 9.5 billion in Special Drawing Rights in the world, but you will never own one, touch one, or even see one.

Although the SDR — as it is called — is the new world money, replacing gold, it exists only as entries in the account books of the International Monetary Fund.

Here are some questions and answers about the SDR. (Q) What is an SDR worth? (A) About $1.20 in U.S. dollars. It originally was worth $1.00 but the two official dollar devaluations have changed this. (Q) Who says it is world money? (A) The International Monetary Fund, an organization of 126 non-communist countries that regulates financial transactions between countries. It created the SDR in 1969 to increase the amount of world funds. (Q) What can I buy with an SDR; what is its importance to me? (A) You won't ever have an SDR to spend. They exist only on the record books of the IMF. But it is important to you because the governments can pay their bills with them. (Q) What do you mean by paying bills? (A) Well, if a country buys a million dollars worth of U.S. wheat and doesn't have the cash to pay for it, it can settle up in SDR's. (Q) Well, if I'm a U.S. wheat farmer, doesn't that mean that I get the SDR's? (A) No, either the U.S. government or the government of the other country will exchange the SDR's to another country for cash, when the cash is needed. Some countries don't need the cash, and let their SDR's accumulate. Beginning July 1, they will earn 5 per cent interest. (Q) How does a country obtain its SDR's? (A) About $9.5 billion in SDR's were distributed by the I.M.F. according to a rigid formula in 1970, 1971, and 1972. They have not been distributed since because there is no pressing need for more, except in developing countries. In addition, there is some disagreement over how they should be used. (Q) What's the disagreement? (A) Well, under the old formula—based on a nation's contribution to the I.M.F.—the developing nations received only small amounts of SDR's, while the industrial nations got the lion's share. The developing nations want a bigger share, at no extra cost, that they would use for development purposes. The issue is known as the "SDR-link."

The United States and West Germany would end up exchanging cash for the SDR's for the developing world, and they are reluctant to do this. The U.S. government thinks that it would be inflationary and that it would be a form of foreign aid which the U.S. Congress would have no control. (Q) What's this about a new value for the SDR? (A) The IMF's committee of twenty — a group of world finance ministers including U.S. Treasury Secretary William E. Simon — agreed this week to base the SDR's value on a package of 16 world currencies. The U.S. dollar will contribute most to the value — about 33 per cent. (Q) How was the SDR valued before? (A) Its value was based on the U.S. dollar, whose value in turn, was based on gold. But when the U.S. decided against paying its international debts in gold in 1971, it made the value of the SDR quite unstable, causing its fortunes to rise and fall with the dollar. By mixing together a basket of currencies, the value of the SDR will not have to be dependent on the fortunes of a *single currency. (Q) Does gold have any remaining role in the monetary system? (A) The United States hopes not. It feels that gold prices are unstable and inflationary. Official gold reserves of western nations and the IMF have been unused for some time. But we did agree this week to let countries with financial problems use their gold as collateral for international borrowing." (3).*

That was the end of the release. Well my friends, there is the SDR story from beginning to end. Please read it well because it contains so many keys to what the one-worlders have up their collective sleeves and what they have planned for us. It is especially noteworthy to remember that after all of that rhetoric about this new non-money money, that the last sentence of the article states that they still do agree that gold will be the only item of security collateral on the international open money market. They've got our silver and they are after our gold ! The SDR — a new non-money money that will eliminate money as we now know and understand it to be and function. This international monopolist's trick will gain for them complete control of the international markets and will continue the heavy drain on our already over-burdened economy, if it achieves its stated goals. I hope this part of the article hit home the plan behind the plan to you?

"The IMF Committee of 20 — a group of world finance ministers including William F. Simon (4) — agreed this week to base the SDR's value on a package of 16 world currencies. The U.S. dollar will contribute most to the value — about 33 per cent."

Here we go again on another financial roller-coaster ride. Just who is it who has been empowered to speak for the American public in the financial councils of the world? I do not know who has been voted that power but I well know who has usurped it — the McNamara's and the other Rothschilds and Rockefellers agents who are once again rushing us headlong into their devious one-world power schemes, that's who ! ! But more has to be done. Progress for the plotters is painfully slow.

You and I, Mr. and Mrs. Ordinary America still stand in the path of their actual physical take-over of our country. We are the last bastion of defense for our beleaguered freedoms, and our enemies well know it.

According to the World Book Encyclopedia, the World Bank deals in lending money for large governmental projects. The International Monetary Fund on the other hand adjusts the differences between the money systems used by the various countries, making it easier for the countries to trade with one another. And these tools of the international monopolists from within, are being used to the disadvantage of America. I am not advocating that we should not help other nations during their periods of famine and other natural disaster. Rather I am stating that we need to re-examine our role as a welfare source for the far-flung corners of this earth and to consider the sageness of the fact that charity should begin at home. After emergency relief, it seems to me that the helping hands many other nations seek, will best be found at the ends of their own collective arms, not stretched across the oceans, as it often the case now.

At this time when our nation is deep in the throes of serious economic problems, I am advocating that we need to turn our full attention to the salvation of our own faltering financial solidarity, before we have to face the reality of extended soup lines again. I am also seriously questioning our continuing role as international developer and as world policemen. We have more than ample need to develop our own resources and economy and the rampant crime in our many urban areas cries for a few policemen and enforcement solutions of their own.

It just seems to me that we could well use some of the easily flowing billions of dollars we now spend in this international development to solve some of our own national problems. It seems to me that concern about the serious situation in our own back yard should certainly receive top priority over our concern and continuing intervention in the problems of the rest of the world. Of what benefit will it be if we continue to clean-up and develop the rest of the world, as our own nation deteriorates and crumbles under the weight of a national apathy? Do we wish to be known as the late, great country of America? I don't and I don't think that the vast majority of Americans do either. But many of the Rhodes-scholar type, socialistically-oriented spokesmen and leaders seem hell-bent on making such our young nation's fate.

I think that you and I, the former Mr. and Mrs. Silent Majority, have got a totally different idea about what the future of this great land must be. Whatever our problems are, we can face them squarely and find solutions. We can roll up our sleeves, use some good old American discipline and beat these pollution problems. We can sit down as mature men of good faith and solve the racial dilemma that has beset our land. We can pull in our belts a few notches and conquer this inflationary/recession roller-coaster we are now strapped into. We can do all of these things and we can solve any other problem, major or minor, which looms on our national horizon as a creative and industrious nation of freedom loving folks.

But right now, we need to send a clean mandate to the seat of federal power, the U.S. government in Washington, D.C., and to every state and local bureaucracy now empowered by our votes. We must let them know that we are sick and tired of mismanagement, rampant spending programs, and of official misconduct. Elected officials are the servants of the people and that specific order of priority must be reestablished. Let me repeat that all important statement — ELECTED OFFICIALS ARE THE SERVANTS OF THE PEOPLE. We must no longer tolerate a group of malicious, star-studded tyrants, enamoured of their own importance, driving us into international situations that threaten our way of life — overtly and not covertly. We need no more expensive, publicity-grabbing junkets to Red China and the Riviera alike, at the tax-payers expense. If they want to run all around the world, let them pay for it out of their five and six figured salaries. Public officials must end the practice of becoming millionaires while in office. They are being paid to serve, not amass fortunes. We need to develop some statesmen and sincere public servants, not a bunch of jet-setting "pretty-people." There was an article recently in a national magazine about the antics of a New York State Senator's wife who was so far out into her "pretty-people" myth, that even the new "anything-goes-disco's" are too staid for her jaded tastes. Besides her obvious sickness, is that the kind of people I want representing me and America? My answer is a resounding no ! !

We need concerned politicians to address themselves to the problems of our youth and their lowering standards of education, toward the elimination of the sub-culture among so many of our disillusioned youth. We need representatives who are prepared to meet the challenge of America today and to come up with solutions to our local and our national problems, solutions that are formed out of a genuine dedication and love for our land.

I think that most of us are tired of rebuilding a largely ungrateful world at large, at the terrible expense of weakening ourselves. Charity begins at home and I think it is high time that some of our duly elected officials got that message, loud and clear. We, the people, are tired of sticking our muscle-bound, protective noses into other people's problems, especially when their problems do not concern our well-being in the least. Vietnam should be the last no-win war that we ever participate in around this world. If something does not directly threaten our shores or our people, we should not get involved. The mid-east, near-east, far-east, and Europe should be told to solve their own international and intranational squabbles. The last young valiant Americans blood should have drained into foreign soil for geopolitical causes which have little or nothing to do with our well-being and safety.

A recent Harris poll shows that 59 per cent of the American people are unhappy with the state of our nation. 79 per cent feel that the rich get richer and that the poor get poorer, regardless of the industry and labor expended. A vast majority of our fellow citizens stated a definite disenchantment with the way our country is run and what effects it is having on plain American lives. It is a clear case of the tail wagging the dog when we have a vast majority of the citizens unhappy with conditions and the dogmatic elected politicians seemingly content to continue down the same suicide path of political and economic chaos that is largely to blame for middle America's unhappiness.

Another recent survey conducted by the Institute for International Social Research, an affiliate of John Hopkins University, established that a majority of the American public now holds isolationist views. (5). The results of the poll states that there has been a dramatic shift in attitudes in the past two years. The trend appears to have taken place in every major segment of the population, but it has been most dramatic, by far, in the lower income and educational group of America. This startling and rapid change has taken place since Nixon has stressed his policy of new relations with China and the Soviet Union. Apparently the average American citizen does not buy detente' nor the official stance Washington has assumed. For a public figure who made his initial national impact as the avowed enemy of communists agent Alger Hiss, Richard M. Nixon took some very odd directions in recent times.

Add to all of this disenchantment the disclosure that Chase Manhattan Bank, Bank of America, and he National City Bank of N.Y., three of America's largest and lending rate here in America at this writing varies from the past year, in order to establish branch offices in Moscow, Russia. It seems the federal government has decided that it is all right for certain large American firms to do business with Russia, and these three banks want a piece of the action. The cause for your concern is valid when you ponder how total seems to be our official and financial capitulation to these, our avowed foes. Could it be that these financial giants have some insider information, much like Bernard Baruch had in 1928 which makes Moscow the place to be for the heavy money action of the future?

As always seems to be the case, we extend to the Soviets a generosity that is lacking at home. The prime lending rate here in America at this wriing varies from 10% to a top of about 12%. The Soviets are borrowing untold millions of our dollars (which incidently are dollars you have deposited in banks, which are used for loans) from these three Moscow-based financial institutions at a fixed rate of 7%, over a guaranteed rate period of ten years. Pretty nice for them. Very unfair to us.

It seems to mean, once again, that our charity should begin at home. If prime interest rates are going to be lowered to favor anyone, why shouldn't it be for American businessmen, the person who has, through industry and creativity, created the jobs for many millions of other Americans. I am sure that Russian truck factories and huge chemical fertilizer complexes, are vital to a healthy *Soviet* economy, but I am equally sure (and the polls are bearing me out) that the average American no longer wishes to be the financial angels for such communistic ventures, when we have ever-lengthening lines of the unemployed on our own shores.

Chase Manhattan Bank, like all banks, operates with the funds with which we, the people, entrust them. It is our hard-earned capitalistic cash which is flowing through these banks into the coffers of the Kremlin, and we, who are aware of that fact, do not approve of it one little bit.

Already on occasion, one can read small news stories about small tenant farmers in rural Mississippi testing the durability of Russian produced tractors on their farms. For what? Are we saying that we cannot produce enough such machines nationally to meet the needs of our farm communities? Or is this just another part of our continuous attitudenal acceptance testing? Will we soon be run off the network of federal highways by an influx of cheap, slave-labor produced Russian tractors and trucks also? So the countdown to depression continues, at a steady pace, into our daily lives from many differing fronts. The assault is constant. The name of the game is power, and America and the Americans, the prize. The World Bank and I.M.F. are playing their roles well.

Nelson Rockefeller greets Khrushchev, the infamous "Butcher of Budapest." The Rockefeller and Eaton families have now joined forces to build war production plants behind the Iron Curtain so that the Communists can become a bigger threat to U.S. survival. America spends $70 billion a year ostensibly on defense and then the Rockefellers build aluminum mills for the Communists.

Lord Alfred Milner, wealthy Englishman and front man for the Rothschilds, served as paymaster for the international bankers in Petrograd during the Bolshevik Revolution. Milner later headed secert society known as The Round Table which was dedicated to establishing a world government whereby a clique of superrich financiers would control the world under the guise of Socialism. The American subsidiary of this conspiracy is called the Council on Foreign Relations.

According to his grandson John, Jacob Schiff (above), long-time associate of the Rothschilds, financed the Communist Revolution in Russia to the tune of $20 million. According to a report on file with the State Department, his firm, Kuhn Loeb and Co. bankrolled the first five year plan for Stalin, Schiff's partner and relative, Paul Warburg, engineered the establishment of the Federal Reserve System while on the Kuhn Loeb payroll.

(1) "None Dare Call It Conspiracy," page #85

(2) Besides giving away huge amounts of our national wealth, we also supplied most of those nations with their initial know-how in technical production, and marketing skills, which allowed their economic recovery to come about so swiftly.

(3) Las Vegas Review-Journal, 23 June, 1974

(4) William F. Simon, the former Nixon-appointed federal energy czar, who ordered and carried out the wasteful printing of billions of rationing coupon before the myth of the energy hoax was exposed on national TV by King Hussein of Jordan, in a visit to America, during the height of the manufactured crisis.

(5) Taken from a Los Angeles Times article about Lloyd A. Free, the author of a think-tank book entitled "A Nation Observed," published by Potomic Associates.

Chapter Six

THE TACTIC OF PRESSURE

Earlier in the book I promised to get back to the socialistic tactic of exerting pressure from both ends, top and bottom, against the middle to achieve their ends here in America. I told of socialist/communist dominated labor unions forever demanding higher and higher prices for the workers, while competitive imports were being sold at half the price. Several other "warning" books have discussed this tactic in detail, but I think it important enough to include it in this book also. You see the workers who would strike to get the higher wages did not realize that they were playing right into the hands of the enemy, nor did they realize the severe consequences their actions would cause in supposedly unrelated areas of the economy. But the labor union officials who were agents for socialism/communism were well aware of the total consequences of the seemingly isolated actions they undertook. The constant demands led to the early manifestations of the inflationary period we now all suffer as a result. Many of the wages earned today are unrealistically high and they in no small part, are causing the inflationary spiral to soar ever higher. The truth is the light. That is pressure from the bottom.

I will try to show still another manner in which this tactic is used to try and force America into the grand design of one-world-ism. I think we all understand and agree how important education is to the future of our country. It is through education that our children are formed, and through those who pursue higher education, that the leadership and the literary directions of our future are formed. As a result, education is one of the main targets for the one-world agents in America.

One of the main areas which those who would take our liberties away concentrate on, is in the field of education.

They are well aware that those who teach the young, shape the future. Since they want the future to be one of socialistic oneness, they go to great lengths to gain access and inroads into our schools. Just as the young Rhodes was impressed and formed by the teachings of Ruskin, so are the Angela Davis' and the many other well-publicized contemporary socialist/communist radicals, influenced and urged on by their teachers and professors in schools, colleges, and universities around the world. They select and isolate the brightest students and fill their minds with the dogma of the far left. These impressionable minds are then propagandized into the channels of thought which these socialist-oriented instructors desire.

In order to get into these teaching positions, if any resistance is offered, they apply the pressure from the top, pressure from the bottom tactic. This is how a typical example would work. I have shown how the international financial establishments have chosen the socialist/communist movement to accomplish their goals of a one-world supra-government. As pointed out in the revelation of their financial backing for the revolutions and take-overs by this group, they have done this most probably because they think that they (the communists) are best suited to the task of breaking the will of the people to resist, and as such, the transition from the dictatorial powers of the communist police state to the big-brother totalitarianism rule they seek, will be smoothest and easiest for them in their quest for power. They envision no pockets of resistance nor armed conflict when the time comes for their take-over. A few select assassinations of a few of their former partners in crime and the task will be finished, according to their plans.

Now, many of these same big money sources are the financial main-stays for most of our institutions of higher learning. As such, they are the life blood of the advanced educational system. It is this undeniable factor which gains them the inroads and the leverage they seek in controlling these institutions. As the chief benefactors, if the President of a given school puts up any opposition to a leftist instructor coming into the school, they tighten up on the purse strings of their grants and endowments, while talking loftily of academic freedoms. The President has to give in or face the loss of some of the needed financial aid necessary to continue the school's operation. Sometimes the opposition is stubborn and then the socialists simply enlist the aid of their well-organized cadre forces and shock troops, to go out and mingle with the students and then to foment unrest and most probably, a series of well publicized protests on the campus. The students, being young, full of energy, and impressionable, are generally easily enlisted in such causes. The battle cry becomes "censorship" and/or "freedom in learning" and the protest banners are held high by the serious but unsuspecting students, who are really dupes and pawns for the plotters in their never-ending quest to control us.

Caught between the threat of the loss of monetary support from the top and the resulting Board of Regents pressure, the chanting mobs of vocal students applying public opinion pressure from the streets below, the hapless President (or Chairman of a Department as the case may be) is a person without a chance to win. As the faculty becomes more and more socialistically-oriented, all the other teachers are forced to watch the molding of the curricula in a manner calculated to give aid and comfort to the one-worlders. Have you read any textbooks recently? Generally it is very disheartening to see how history and attitudes have been twisted and shaped to fit the one-world thinking. All of this means that the sponge-like minds of the young students are then doomed to the relentless pressure of the socialist-oriented manners of thinking. The utopian rhetoric is a part of the education which we serve up to our finest young minds. Our future leaders, educators, scientists, artists, and business people are all given to believe that the left-orientation is both harmless to their future and a correct way of life. You can see just how serious the plot is and how deadly the results we suffer. Like so many other walks of American life, our educational system has been skillfully and dogmatically infiltrated by the agents of an alien ideology and they are now in a position to control our future thought processes. The result, dedicated communists are being turned into our streets annually as a result of this folly? It is a situation which loyal Americans need to address themselves to immediately.

Another recent classic example of the pressure tactic may be found in the so-called energy crisis. Let me assure you that I am not saying that there is not cause for alarm and for conservation in the area of naural energy sources here in America. What I am stating is that the late winter 1973 - early spring 1974 deprivations that most Americans suffered were both unnecessary and a hoax. I state unequivically that the vast wealth of evidence now available shows that the international oil companies did conspire to make Americans think that a world energy famine was full upon us. They sold us this concept and made us accept this as fact and to move on to the next step of energy-belt-tightening and then seeking alternative sources of fuel.

What really happened was that the American/International oil cartels wanted to realize even greater profits from their products than they could gain under prevailing conditions. The federal government, already smarting under mounting public criticism for the favored-status legislation given these same oil groups, imposed implied ceilings on the constant price increases of petroleum and petroleum products. It was then that these international financial powers began to apply one of their most successful tactics, the top and bottom ploy, to achieve their goals.

The Arab/Israeli War provided them with the reason they needed. They invented the oil embargo and then, to manufacture the shortages they needed, they held back on the shipment and delivery of their more-than-ample supplies of crude oil. Before the so-called shortage, Americans were loudly complaining about the constant pennies-per-gallon price increases. After a few months of chilly houses and places of work, plus the long waits in lines at service stations for minimum purchases, our stand softened considerably on higher prices. In fact, in a very short period of time, the average American was willing to

pay close to 100% more for gas than they had been paying shortly before. The people of America were given
controls and threats of rationing from the top in response
to the restricted availability pressure on the public from
the bottom. This example is a classic case of the tactic
and the end results were predictable. We now drive con-
fidently up into any gas station again and tell the
attendant to "Fill it up," and all the major oil firms are
reporting profit-increases ranging from 100% to 890%
for the first half of 1974. Those bonanza profits will some-
day help to finance a lot of socialist-inspired infiltration
of our institutions and government.

Occasional stories leaked out into the press during the
shortage of fuel, but few paid heed to them. There were
the reports of fleets of super-tankers anchored off the
eastern seaboard with more than enough oil to meet our
needs. There was the mid-eastern Monarch who revealed
on a live TV interview that during the height of the
crisis, more oil was being exported from the mid-east than
at any time in history. Then there was the recently dis-
charged serviceman who reported that it was his duty in
Vietnam, during the height of the shortage, to burn
hundreds of thousands of gallons of surplus fuel daily,
lest it become an unmanageable burden in the U.S.
supply depots in that far away land. These and a few
other stories like them appeared in print; but we were
too chilly and too fearful about the spector of rationing
to pay much attention to the constant hints that the entire situation may have been manufactured. Because of
our demonstrated willingness to go along with the 'crisis,'
some international energy cartels are getting very, very
wealthy these days.

Should I mention again that Prince Bernhard's own
financial fortunes are tied to the fortunes of Dutch Shell,
one of the international oil firms. I have repeatedly
pointed out that Bernhard is at the head of the Bilderberg
Group, which is the modern day inner-circle of the Round
Table conspirators. So it is much like a jig-saw puzzle.
The more pieces that I put in front of you, the more you
can see that they will fit together in one big picture of

scheming and conspiracy. The top and bottom pressure tactic of the recent energy crisis benefited the one-worlders, as do the inroads they make into our educational institutions. I have shown you that these same forces are those who have vowed to destroy our way of life and rule us.

Chapter Seven

ARE COMMODITIES GOING UP OR, ARE CURRENCIES GOING DOWN?

In the year 1940, we had, by dint of patient work and native ingenuity, very slowly overcome the crippling blow which the '29 crash and the ensuing depression had caused. During 1940 one dollar in U.S. currency would buy ten loaves of bread. In 1974 one dollar in U.S. currency will now buy only two loaves of bread. But note in 1974 a silver dollar will still purchase ten loaves of bread, because in 1974 a real silver dollar can be exchanged for five paper dollars. That little example is a simple lesson in inflation, devaluation, and real values. It is meant to prove that value is constant and that it is only the governmental value system which fluctuates and varies, not real value. It also proves that in a very real sense, the U.S. currency is now one-fifth the value that it was in 1940. Another way of putting it is that the dollar has devalued to twenty cents (.20) in 1974 compared to 1940. The items and things of real and lasting value, like metal monetary units (silver and gold), are very constant. It may seem (according to the governmental economists) that the silver dollar is inflated since it is now worth five times what is was in 1940. But upon careful examination we will find that the silver dollar will still purchase the same ten loaves of bread that it would in 1940. That is consistancy.

An example of false devaluation and economic savings would be when a retailer raises all of the prices in his store by twenty percent and then advertises that he is holding a storewide sale, with discounts up to twenty per cent. In truth nothing has changed but the basic price on the items price tags.

If the government would tell the truth about the inflation we are suffering, it is quite possible that we could muster some of our "good-ole-American" ingenuity and come up with some workable solutions to the problem. But at the end of each quarter year, when the governmental agencies solemnly announce the inevitable price and wage increases, they always have a manufactured reason why this or that happened. They go on to state that the inflationary spiral has been contained and should now start to recede. Then at the next reporting period they make the same solemn announcements and the vicious cycle continues. The truth is, what with the endless rounds of price increases, which are always preceeded or followed by the labor demands for cost-of-living increases-plus, a solution is further away now than at any time in recent history. Perhaps it is true that we will never again return to the era of the ten-cent loaf of bread, but it does not mean that we have to continue in the age of the fifty-cent loaf of bread either. The truth is that inflation is a *hidden tax* imposed on the American public by the federal government. But they will never admit to this, and that just adds to the entire problem.

The people know that something is gravely wrong in our country and that is why inflation has now replaced corruption and crime as the number one concern of the American public. The hidden tax concept makes even more sense when you stop to consider that this tactic follows the concepts set down by our avowed enemies, as one needed to help defeat us.

Karl Marx stated many times that one of the most effective ways to destroy the bourgeoisie was through the institution of, and constant pressure from, a progressive and unrelenting program of taxation. Is that not what is being done today? Those monies that the ever-higher taxes do not legally confiscate out of hard-earned incomes, are inflation-taxed away from us. The working-class, middle-class are beleaguered in America today. This situation did not just occur; it is a part of the grand design to wear us down and to eventually rule us.

There are many official federal policies which make these conditions possible. The greatest of these citizen-

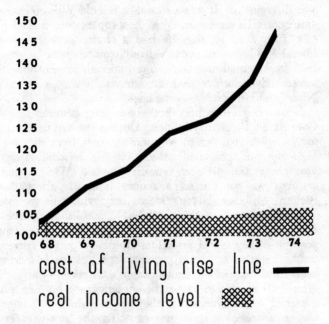

cost of living rise line ▬
real income level ▨

oppressing conditions is the official Keynesian economic policy that was adhered to by the Nixon administration. Richard M. Nixon was elected to the Presidency by the electorate who believed his conservative election promises. We really believed that his administration would return to more·conservative directions in national and international policies, as he had promised in the campaign. The ever-broader liberal policies of several administrations prior to the election of Nixon had convinced the majority that a new outlook was needed in Washington.

Once elected, Richard M. Nixon proved to be the biggest spender of them all. He embarked on a career of out-spending both the gentlemen from Texas and the gentleman from Massachusetts. He also seemed hell-bent on out-involving us internationally, which was contrary to what the masses had indicated that they wanted. Once empowered, the Mitchells and the Kissingers took over the running of the ship of state, and the will of the people was disregarded. It was a repeat of the old Wilson/Roosevelt saga all over again. We, the people, were tricked by talk, into thinking that he had a choice between ultraliberal McGovern or conservative Nixon when in fact they both represented the same international powers and interests. Even before that time it was a choice between Nixon and Humphrey. Some choice.

Nixon and Humphrey both have long histories in the Council on Foreign Relations. During the campaign oratory, they verbalized their common goals from diametrically opposed points of view. America rejected Hubert Humphrey and his socialistically inspired ADA supporters, but we got the same actions from the alternative, Richard Milhouse Nixon. Heads they win, tails we lose.

It is because of this high-level established political duplicity and actual non-choice that I have taken my position of support of an actual alternative to our current political quagmire. I am proudly a part of the fast-rising grass-roots supported Independent American Party, a group of unabashed patriotic Americans who are not ashamed to announce that they relish both our freedom and our free enterprise system. To the one-worlders, capitalism means monopolism. I say that socialism and communism are the really nasty words and we need to be unafraid to say that in public. Unfortunately both of our traditional political parties are infested with Council-on-Foreign Relations types and other representatives of the international economic plotters. They gnaw away at the fabric of our Republic and it is up to us to stop them.

In order to have any real choice when we go to the polls in the future, we need a party which represents the wants and the needs of the plain citizen, those strong-willed people who have built this nation into the power it now is, just as the traditional parties now represent those power-brokers of one-world-ism. Please understand that I am not talking about the precinct-level, grass-roots workers. To a great extent they are honest, hard-working folks who are trying to make the system work. But they have been betrayed by the leadership of their respective

The boss and his two employees — the three musketeers of the CFR — Rocky, President Nixon and Henry Kissinger confer. Kissinger of Harvard was made virtual Assistant President by Rockefeller on whose staff he had served for a dozen years. Kissinger also had been on the staff of the CFR just prior to joining the Nixon Administration. Kissinger was the very embodiment of everything Nixon denounced during his '68 campaign. This explains why Nixon reversed himself on so many stands.

Home of the Council on Foreign Relations on 68th St. in New York. The admitted goal of the CFR is to abolish the Constitution and replace our once independent Republic with a World Government. CFR members have controlled the last six administrations. Richard Nixon had been a member and appointed at least 100 CFR members to high positions in his administration.

parties and somebody needs to say it. There is not a dimes worth of difference getween the leaders of the Democrat and the Republican parties in America today.

I certainly hope to continue the proud Houston tradition of making a concrete contribution to America. I also hope that many sincere Americans will feel the need for a real choice at the polls, and that they will go and investigate for themselves what the Independents are talking about. If they do this, I am sure that many will opt for a political party which is dedicated to the idea that the best government is the least government and that elected officials should once again serve the needs of the majority of the people. The Independent American Party awaits with open arms and hearts all the citizens who want to return America to Americans.

Back to Nixon. Once settled in the White House, former President Nixon returned to the advice of his selected economic advisors. They turned to the dictates of the god-father of non-money money, John M. Keynes. This direction was in direct opposition to the Nixon campaign promises. Let us turn to this man Keynes and try to see who and what he was. According to the encyclopedia, John Maynard Keynes (Baron Keynes of Tilton) lived from 1883 until 1946. Because of his writings and theories, he has become one of the most influential economists of all time. He authored many books on the economy and the book, "General Theory of Employment, Interest, and Money," (1936) changed the economic theories and policies of many western nations today. In his writings Keynes analyzed depressions and gave his formula for avoiding them. His remedy was to print more and more paper money and then get it into general circulation via government programs. He totally disregarded the need to back up such money with silver or gold.

The basis of Keynesian economics is deceptively simple. Keynes states that the level of economic activity depends on the total spending of consumers, business, and government. If consumer activity was minimal and business was poor, Keynes urged increased government spending programs and easy money through the availability of loans and low-interest rates. According to Keyne's analysis, it was shown that high levels of demand were essential for employment and economic growth, even if these levels were artificial. We now have first-hand experience in America on how well this theory does *not* work. It is the old story of theory versus practice. The market is now and forever shall be decided by the people and false government optimism and inflationary non-money money will never solve the problem.

Keynes was born in Cambridge, England and later studied at the famous university in that city. He served in the British Treasury before becoming a director of the Bank of England in 1941. He was knighted in 1942. That is a thumbnail sketch of the creator of a new economic system which is slowly paralyzing the economic vigor of our capitalistic society. Did you note that he, too, was a Cambridge student? That was where at least half of the Ruskinites were accredited to form the Rhodesian secret society. Like Wilson's 'Colonel' House, Keynes was an Englishman who somehow came into the position to guide our economic fortunes. With that I have added another bit of seemingly unrelated data that seems to fit perfectly into the ever-growing picture of the conspiratorial puzzle. Doesn't it seem strange that with all of America's well-financed and established seats of learning, we are still dependent upon the dictates of the Cambridge system for our economic guidance and directions?

America struck out on its own path and form of government after declaring our independence from England. Our form of government was new and innovative and built upon the faith that together we could do anything that we set our minds to do. Why is it now, after several hundred years of following the dictates of our own minds, it suddenly became necessary for us to seek out and follow the dictates of the Houses and the Keynes and other foreign dictation in our fiscal and other official policies? Of course there is a very logical answer.

When the conspirators found that they could not take America by might they went to work with the sabotaging-America-from-within techniques that have worked so well for them. They infiltrated all areas of importance and have proceeded to do all in their power to destroy our Republic. I have outlined many of the devious schemes in this book but there are many more that I haven't touched upon, that are of equal importance. Religion, entertainment, transportation, and manufacturing are but a few of these very important areas that have not been touched in this book; but the conspirators are at work in each of them with the same deadly devotion and schemes that I have touched upon in finance, government, media, and education. Think of all the socialist-oriented persons whom you can think of in those fields; and remember that to the one-world folks, socialism and communism are interchangeable words. Then consider what a Russian like Alexander Solzhenitsyn would give to be able to write a critical book like this in his native land and then be able to remain there without prosecution and repression. For Solzhenitsyn it is too late. For us there is still time.

Chapter Eight

LIBERALS VS. CONSERVATIVES
WHAT THE LABELS MEAN

The greatest issue of our day is that of personal freedom versus government control.
Those in favor of freedom call themselves
"conservatives"—those who favor maximum
government intervention and control have
appropriated the name "liberals."

The hopes of free men everywhere for the
present and for the indefinite future lie upon
the outcome and the struggle between these
two points of view.

John E. Roche, M.D.

Somewhere in the time period between 1776 and 1974
the mind-manipulators have been able to reverse the true
meaning of conservative, making it unpopular in America.
They have linked the word with a negative connotation
and made many of us shy away from the label. By the
advent of the post-McCarthy era, the real bogey-man
image was firmly implanted with any tag of conservatism.
But let us take another look at this much-maligned word.
What does conservative really mean? It is important for
us to do this, now that we are understanding some of the
forces behind the anti-conservative movement. To con-
serve means to save or to use sparingly, to keep from
harm or to protect from harm or decay. In nature, conservation means the protection of and wise usage for our
natural resources. That somehow doesn't seem like something that I need to be ashamed to be or to be afraid of,
as an American.

The dictionary definition of a political conservative is
a person or party that places a great emphasis on tradi-

tion. It seems that conservatives rely on history as a guide to governmental wisdom and further, they have great respect for historical ideas and institutions. Therefore, they seek progress in line with proven values of the past. Conservatives believe that most political problems are basically moral problems and that it has been proven historically that legislation cannot significantly change the attitudes of mankind. A conservative believes in the greatest amount of free enterprise and a minimal amount of federal government activity into the individual rights of the citizens. We believe that our founding fathers intended that the government should serve the people, not run them.

Prohibition proved, on a national basis, that unpopular legislative acts are the cause of mass disobedience rather than the eventual public submission to those laws. A conservative is not a racist nor a bigot, as a matter of official conservative policy. Like all political parties, I am sure that we have members who follow all types of individual persuasions. However, a conservative believes in equal rights, but believes that these rights should be earned by respect for law and social order, not taken for granted. A conservative is aware that responsibility and restraint are the price we pay for such rights. Conservatives see a necessary link between the enjoyment of liberty and freedom and the institution of the sanctity of private property. We believe that man and woman have a castle in their home and have a right and duty to protect that home from all outside invasions. A conservative is a person who loves freedom and who will die to help protect and preserve liberty. A conservative believes that America is the greatest country on this globe and doesn't wish to trade our form of government for any other that has been created in this world thus far.

From the pieces I have been able to assemble conservative does not sound like someone whom I would be ashamed to be associated with, nor to be called. I, too, believe in the sanctity of individual rights, and I have been outspoken in my opposition to socialistic legislation which is so fashionable today. The war on poverty would have been better named the war against the poverty stricken. Is was and is a bureaucratic boondoggle. Much of this legislation seems to be geared simply to the perpetuation of an increasingly large welfare class in our society. I do not see any humanistic concerns about the future needs of that class and programs designed to realistically bring about their eventual entry into the majority society economically. I am genuinely concerned about the human values and the psychological damage inflicted on people who suffer from economic disorientation. I am worried about the dignity and pride of a welfare mother and the mental emasculation of the welfare father. I am troubled about the consequences on youth who witness the degradation of their parents under that system.

I know many serious people who are caught up in the vise of federal-sponsored welfare programs and most of them would welcome a workable program designed to get them permanently off the welfare roles. But right now, with the bureaucracy involved with the administration of the programs, the welfare group represents job security and a block of votes for the incumbent powers, so they intend to keep these people caught up in the welfare vise. This fact is especially evident in some of the larger cities where payroller-precinct captains demand absolute loyalty from the welfare group, under threat of welfare-check cut-offs to the less than submissive. In many areas we now have third and fourth generation relief recipients, and I am against the perpetuating of that kind of demeaning life style. But I temper my wrath with the realism that three or four generations of wrong cannot be wiped out overnigth, not even with the best intentions.

As an individual who has compassion, I feel that serious social programs in education and training can be sponsored to end these circumstances. The relentless circle of frustration and alienation can be ended. Of course dedication and education is a key to ending the dilemma. I want to see every neighborhood have the finest possible schools and have each offering a standard of excellence and fine education to each and every child all across our nation, bar none. The agony of bussing will be solved when all schools offer educational excellence, and that is what I am for. It seems to me that we are admitting that certain schools are inferior, if, in order to get a decent education, a child has to be bussed away from their own neighborhood schools. So I would make sure that the academic quality of the backbone of the school, the teachers, was outstanding. We cannot have good schools without good teachers. In order to achieve this it will take special efforts in some schools and a consistent effort in others. But it can be done and without the massive funds now expended to bus children all over the country-side. The victims of the current federal bussing laws are the legions of little children who are disoriented daily as they are bussed away from their familiar surroundings and unceremoniously dumped out in other, often hostile neighborhoods. In these locations they are often subjected to indifferent teaching and peer-group resentment and contempt for an entire school career. That experience is causing mental damage we will suffer for years to come.

Conservatives advocate people-oriented programs that do not encompass flowery-phrases. Our problem is to get the word to the people. The one-worlders do not have that problem, since they control most of the media. I believe that the conservative philosophy is a workable solution to our national problems such as the rampant inflation of today and the most probable depression of tomorrow. Since the conservatives are ordinary people it means that the conservatives need you and your input into and support for the programs I am talking about, if such programs are to be given a chance to work for our benefit.

Conservative economics would cut effectively all pork-barrel programs which are now bleeding the American tax-payer dry. We would save billions of dollars annually by ending many of the unnecessary spending programs we now endure. Conservative economics would halt the sumptuous furnishing of congressional offices, the further ordering of unstable and unworkable multi-million dollar warplanes that are outmoded before they are put into production, the total waste involved in the recent gasoline-rationing coupon scandals would end, the world-wide congressional and staff junkets would cease and staffs would be severely restricted, and the whole range of nonsensical but super-high-priced programs would be reviewed.

Why should we continue aid programs to the many hostile countries we now meekly support? Why should we have future stop-opium production programs in Turkey, only to have the growing of the poppy resume after we have paid them millions of dollars to stop? And now we give massive aid to Communist China where opium is a #1 crop. These people must really think us to be fools to continue such nonsense. I think that you get the point I am making, what we need is some representatives of our own people — I am talking about real representatives of the real people — to watchdog over the federal budget and to cut the excess it now contains. Forget about the special interest lobbies and the peddlers of influence, we need some federal-financial soul-searching, and the conservatives can and will do the job if given the opportunity. We have no entrenched interests to serve, no favors to repay.

Do you realize that we have some temporary committees and special groups which were created by Congress to solve the problems of the 1920's back in the 1920's, that are still carried on the federal payroll? There has long since been no justification for their existence, but the bureaucrats on Capitol Hill cannot face the reality of ending the gravey train for their life-long cronies. The hardest thing for a bureaucrat to do is end a bureaucratic program, regardless of the obsolescence of that program. Without fear of rebuttal I can state that at least 25% of the total federal budget could easily be cut, without the loss of any vital or imporant national program. That is quite important when you consider that 25% of our annual budget would mean an immediate savings of almost one-hundred *billion* dollars. Besides the immediate tax savings to the public that this move would men, we would also be cutting the bureaucracy and opportunity for corruption in many areas of the federal operation.

With so many former high-level advisors, cabinet members and sundry highly placed officials either under indictment or already convicted of crimes and corruption in office, the side benefit we gain by cutting the bureaucracy, in addition to the national savings, would in itself be well worth the effort expended. We have to admit that the problem of official corruption is a major one at all levels of government today. I am sure that many books will be written about Watergate and all the tragic consequences it brought about. Many of the main criminals will become wealthy as a result of writing "inside" stories about the shame of that administration and already amnesty is a prime topic of interest throughout our land.

Corruption has assaulted our senses on the national level at such a fever pitch, that we tend to over look crime on the official local level. This is a recent example, found buried way back in the middle pages of one of the local papers:

" . . . A former Justice Department criminal investigator testified to a House subcommittee recently that 'high government officials' are involved in narcotics traffic, bribery, and other forms of crime and corruption along the U.S.-Mexican border, a spokesman for a N.Y. Congressman said." (1)

We must root the bad apples out of the barrel before we lose the entire barrel. Because of the current assault we have endured on our traditional moral standards — I have shown you two more steps in our countdown — the gross bureaucratic over-spending of our tax dollars for programs of no real consequence and the wide-spread official misconduct of elected and appointed officials while holding offices of public trust. Need I speculate where the encouragement and possibly the entrapment leading to these assaults on our moral sensibilities originated? I think that by now you know as well as I who stands to gain most by the continuation of this degeneration.

(1) Las Vegas Review-Journal, 28 June, 1974, page 2.

Chapter Nine

I REST MY CASE - IT IS NOW UP TO YOU — THE AMERICAN JURY — TO DECIDE THE COURSE THAT AMERICA MUST TAKE!

In the many pages and chapters in this book I have outlined what has evolved out the initial Ruskin concept, which he derived from the ideas of Plato, concerning a super-world government. Step by step, however brief it may have been, we have journeyed through the maize of deceptions and intrigues which have led up to our current moral and economic dilemma. We have traveled the path our nation took in the First World War, around the League of Nations, right back into the Second World War, and finally, into the gigantic spider web known as the United Nations, which was both conceived and is controlled by the international monopolists. I have shown the complicity of the Rhodes scholars, of the foreign universities, of the Rothschild finpolitans, and how the members of the Council on Foreign Relations are all part of the plot, in the vast network of the planners for a one-world government.

I have named Morgans and the Rockefellers and the multitudes of international bankers who are part of the sinister forces behind most of the socialist and communist revolutions on a global scale. Finally, and most important, I have pinpointed Prince Bernhard and the Bildenberg Group as the modern-day commanders and theoreticians behind the current one-world Round Table drive for power. Throughout these revelations have popped up such unlikely villains like trusted advisor of Presidents Bernard Banuch and most of our all-American oil cartels. They have been unmasked as part of the plot and the plotters who plan to take away our coveted liberty. The bit players and pawns in the drama, like Nixon and Kennedy, are placed in correct perspective, as I tried to bring to the fore the major characters in this whole rotten mess, characters like Henry Kissinger, the one-worlder's current fair-haired boy. Of the many things that a critic of this effort may decide to say about these works, he cannot truthfully say that I was timid or backed off of my original pledge to name the names, face the facts and to let the chips fall where they may. I have faithfully kept that pledge. That is the conservatives way of facing a problem, facing it squarely and without deception. I feel that it is time for bold and brave actions on the part of all Americans to save our country, and this book is a part of my efforts to galvanize my friends, and neighbors, and you, my fellow Americans into action against a very devious foe.

I am a patriotic person who wishes to see my land and our way of life survive this terrible onslaught which has been unleashed upon us. I am of the blood of known historic patriots and I know, based upon their deeds and actions, that we can survive the menace if we will rally and meet this threatening danger head on before the conspirators have completely enfeebled us and successfully locked us in the shackles of slavery.

The attempt a few years ago to legislate away our rights to bear arms was just another part of the plot to lessen the ability of the American public to resist. Their more successful attempt to have all gun owners register is a thinly veiled attempt to pin-point the potential location of any potential fighters for our basic freedoms. Like prohibition, Mr. and Mrs. America did not comply on a national scale to this unneeded law which would deny us the traditional liberty and rights of self-protection. As a popular bumper-sticker of that time so succinctly stated, "When guns are outlawed, only outlaws will have guns." There is a vast difference between the solid, well-made hand gun which the average citizen has a right to own and to protect life, limb, and property with, and the imported, foreign-made cheap saturday-nite specials which the criminal element favors. Effective legislation to end the import of that kind of weapon still has not been drawn up nor passed. The Kennedy assassination brought about a flood of rhetoric, but today, a full decade or more later, the parts to these deadly saturday-nite specials are still knowingly shipped into the country daily. They are then assembled in murky little factories and then offered for sale to anyone who has the money to purchase them.

To force or to expect a protection-or sports-minded citizen to declare the manner and the extent of his ability to protect his family and his home is to ask that person to be vulnerable to any and all who may eventually have access to those public records and files. My opposition to intra-national surveillance by our professional and military intelligence agencies is based along these same lines. Only those people and/or organizations proven to be agents of a foreign power should even be considered for that kind of scrutiny. All other problems are within the jurisdiction of the local police forces and should so remain, on the local level.

I am equally opposed to the technical-age phenomena of the large computerized invasions of personal privacy, for the benefit of a few credit-extending agencies and institutions. These credit information banks are a dangerous intrusion into the rights of privacy of the individual. A person's credit history should be a valued part of his private business. This knowledge should be exchanged only with the parties full understanding and cooperation, to those firms which he chooses. It is not that way today. Anyone from a former spouse to a potential kidnapper can gain inside financial knowledge of any individual who is on one of these mega-lists. Most of us are on those lists whether we know it or like it or not. All the person seeking this knowledge has to do is to know how to gain access. As a conservative I value individual rights very highly and resent the impersonal liberties taken by both governmental and private sources, regarding such information. All of this random data gathering is very dangerous and needs to be halted.

In a recent article by Washington columnist, Tom Tiede, Herb Philbrick, perhaps the most famous contemporary American counter-spy, states that we have good cause for alarm today. With the emergence of the super-radical groups like the Weathermen and the SLA, we tend to forget the ever-present and more serious threat from communism. Mr. Philbrick warns us that these misled radicals are little more than shock-troops for the ever-present communists. They (the radicals) are paid for and urged on by our true enemies. While our attention is diverted to their deadly antics, the real enemy quietly continue on toward their never-changing goals. In this period of official detente', many of our citizens are confused as to our own role and to the role of the communists. If this confused trend continues, Mr. Philbrick warns, we will look up one day and be involved in a life and death struggle that we truly cannot win. I totally agree with this proven patriot and expert's opinion, and he certainly should know, since he risked his life for many years on the other side of the plotting fence, in devotion to America.

My solutions to our problems, economic and otherwise, are so very simple that they generally tend to be overlooked in the search for solutions. We live in a very complex world and simple answers have a way of mystifying us. First and foremost we must have more people participation in the process of selection and the subsequent election of our various public officials. This is from the local level all the way up to and including the highest federal levels. We need officials who will sincerely represent the wants and the needs of the grass-roots majority and who will end the practice of representing those special interest and lobbies who can exert the most pressure or pay the most money into the political kitty. Milk lobbies and IIT can only happen when the electorate becomes apathetic.

America needs a wholesome wind-down of the many federal spending programs. This is in addition to the complete ending of obsolete and other non-essential programs we also now suffer. We need to end the unlimited powers of the federal government and to cut back federal intervention into the problems of the states and local communities. This would allow the local and the state governments to re-assume their respective roles as an extension of the voice and the will of the people. We need local government that is truly representative of the will and needs of the surrounding community. By a lessening of the spending programs at all levels, much of the current need for excessive taxes and the ensuing pressures on the tax payers would end. Then the earned dollar would stretch much farther in the meeting of our daily needs and in our savings programs, rather than disappearing into the tax coffers. How many of you can remember when a person saved for their retirement years and didn't depend upon social security nor pension funds? Not many, I'll bet. Neither can I; but I have it from very reliable sources that senior citizens were not eating dog food or going cold in the winter, during those days of capitalistic self-sufficiency. Many of the promises of the socialistic scheme do not seem to work out in real life as they do in theory while on paper. That is why all those grandiose five-year plans and the like, are always falling short of their goals. Unfortunately, many persons now giving to social security will find out that brutal fact when the saturation point is reached some time soon. As I have repeatedly pointed out in this book, our system is imperfect, and well do we know it; but it is head and shoulders above whatever is in second place when it comes to a way of life for the benefit of the great majority of our citizens.

I advocate the rewarding of individual industry, which means an end to the progressive tax structure which now penalizes the go-getters in our society. A revamping, from top to bottom, of our entire IRS system is called for as soon as possible, to end the injustice of that bureaucracy. I am for the government getting out of competition with private industry, such as the quasi-public postal system. If the bureaucrats cannot run it profitably, turn the opportunity over to come competent private businessmen who can. It is just that simple. Postmaster Generals will have to give up living like royalty and get down to the business of business, or step aside.

I believe that the general market should allow the natural rhythms of the marketplace to price all commodities offered for sale in that market. I do not believe in government support nor government ceilings. I believe that we need to end the practice of governmental interference in this normal process and the resulting false markets that occurr when there is federal intervention. The recent beef-support efforts and legislation is a good example of this kind of government intervention. Lockheed, Penn-Central, and now Pan Am. are examples of unfair government subsidies to faltering industries. If they can't run them, let them step aside and allow someone who thinks they can, try. I notice that none of the five and six figure salary executives gave up any fraction of their ample salaries to help try and save the business. The buying public and the natural market place have far more sense about price levels, than a whole gaggle of government economic experts, who try to set false levels to fit the economic needs of the empowered administrations.

I advocate the removal of this bogus non-money money which the government has flooded into the market, trying to drown the problems of inflation. As I outlined in the prelude to this book, I think the immediate solution would be the institution of my proposed dual monetary system. Allowing the market the right to find its own level would solve the current inflationary problem, if we had the choice of the two currencies. I further believe that all Americans should have the right to own any amount of any precious metal and/or commodity that are offered in the general marketplaces of the world. This means silver coins, silver bars, gold coins, gold bars, platinum bars, rubies, and diamonds, plus any other commodity that is of personal value to the owner. Any other policy is dictatorial to say the least.

For immediate personal safety of savings wealth and peace of mind I advocate that all Americans convert their wealth to monetary metals. If we do not head off this depression that lies at the end of this repression, the monetary metal will retain the basic value (remember the story about the silver dollar and the loaves of bread?) and it will afford you and your family the liquid assets that will be needed to weather this fiscal fire storm that is about to embrace our nation. You may, like Bernard Baruch, profit from your investment in the metal, but regardless, you may rest assured that you will not lose your money if held in this ageless form of exchange. The more exotic forms of monetary metal investments are pretty much designed for the collectors and the major buyers. I am addressing this advice to the average small American saver, of from one-to fifty-thousand dollars. There is more liquidity in the metals, the smaller the value, the more easily converted to other assets or commodities. Remember that silver, like the basic liberty of Americans, is something that will be a part of our national fabric just as long as the systems survives and prevails.

My advocations and recommendations are simple and direct common-sense steps that are geared to restore the rights of the individual and are designed to take away much of the unlimited power of the federal government. We must withdraw the false royalty status of our elected officials. Our forefathers left the old countries to escape that form of tyranny. Nowhere in the foundations of our government was it written that all of our top-most officials must become wealthy while serving in public office. Nor is it written that these officials are above the law of the land and can deny their responsibility to answer to the taxpayers for their actions and misdeeds.

The arrogance of an Agnew, who continues to cost us, the taxpayers, many, many dollars in office space and secretarial costs as he travels around the world in quest of more money, is an insult heaped upon the injustice of his slap-on-the-wrist punishment, for his official misconduct. His arrogance is condoned in Washington by his cronies and partners in crime, but it must be made known that we, the people, do not accept this smooth talking corruption any longer.

We must reacquaint ourselves with the hopes, dreams, and concepts as set down for our democratic Republic by our founding fathers. We must update those principles and practices which have worked to the best advantage of the majority. We must hold national referendums to change those ideas which have not worked, and regardless, the voice of the majority of the people must be heard.

We must learn to take an active interest and participate in the functioning of our government, or we will soon not have a people's government in which to participate. We must once again return to the principles which allows other countries to solve their own disputes and problems, as we return to the important job of solving the multitude of our own bureaucratic bumblings.

We must return to the pride of unabashed patriotism and to once again learn to love our land with a total love which will help us to resolve most of the difficult problems which plague our nation. We must depend upon good old American faith and ingeunity to come to the rescue when all else fails. Most important, we must shake off the doledrums of apathy and become activists for the salvation of America today. If we fail to heed the warnings and continue down the paths designed by the one-worlders as a part of their countdown to depression, we may well some day soon, surrender much of our freedom to these conspiratorial forces I have written of on these pages. One final thought: Remember that like charity, action best begins at home, to benefit home. Think about that and do something positive for the preservation of our Republic today — tomorrow just may be too late.

— END —

A Postscript

THE· STATE OF THE NATION

without rose-colored glasses and other forms of self-deception

In pursuing a well-known book recently, I came across a fairly realistic set of guidelines, outlining the obvious national trends and the course of action that our Republic is following during the mid-nineteen-seventies. I shall recount those rules to you now, word for word, letter for letter, with some comments by this author added in the parentheses: (1) Abolition of property and application of all rents to public purpose; (If you will note, the current per hundred-dollar valuation assessment by means of a property tax, in a very real manner means, in effect, that the so-called land owners, the backbone of our entire structure, never really owns the land they are annually taxed to keep. Are they not really renting this property from the taxing authority? If you think that this evaluation is harsh or incorrect, refuse to pay these taxes and find out what happens to "your" land. We both know that it will be quite legally confiscated to satisfy the demands of the tax authority. So what that indicates is that you are paying a year to year rental fee (taxes) and will be evicted if you fail to do so, with the property being re-rented to someone who is willing and able to pay the eternal rent. Unpleasant but true). (2) A heavy progressive or graduated income tax; (I really don't think that the preceeding statement needs any explanation to any tax-paying U.S. citizen. The IRS is the watchdog over a method that systematically penalizes any person, with an ever-increasing amount of severity, according to the amount of industry and success that person achieves. This is the 20% to 90% scale of brackets the IRS has devised, according to the income earned. It is clearly a system of penalizing you for your ability to earn or to succeed). (3) Abolition of all rights of inheritance; (To those unfortunate enough to have experienced a recent non tax-sheltered inheritance, it is a shattering experience to see what happens to the security planned by the departed ones and intended for their loved ones. The inheritance tax is one of the most authoritarian and repressive of all the acts perpetrated upon the American public today. It makes a mockery and shambles of justice). (4) Confiscation of all property of emigrants and rebels; (The best example of this little-considered violation of citizen's rights, because many emigrants do become citizens, is the detention and confiscation of many thousands of Japanese-Americans' property during the second World War; but there are numerous less-publicized and isolated violations occurring annually* (1) (5) Centralization of credit in the hands of the state by means of a national bank with state capital and an exclusive monopoly; (The sinister and devious Federal Reserve Bank System is exactly such an octopus - like federal monopoly.) (6) Centralization of the means of communication and transportation in the hands of the state; (Remember recently when an irked Nixon vowed to make some of his investigative tormentors — specifically the *Washington Post* group of radio/TV interests — pay for their transgressions through a control of their F.C.C. needed relicensing application efforts? Add to that consideration the ever-growing power of the highway-taxed financed I.C.C. and/or the congressional-spawned quasi-public (?) national transportation system that is now called Amtrak, which is little more than a country-wide subsidization and camouflaged nationalization of the railways.) (7) Extension of factories and instruments of production owned by the state, bringing the cultivation of waste lands and the improvement of the soil generally in accordance wih a common plan; (This category has so many applications, it is hard to select one or two, to make the point. There are the industrial subsidies — millionaire's welfare — to Penn-Central and/or Lockheed, or the agricultural subsidies in the form of artificial-price support levels or the soil-bank programs. In addition, there is the Bureau of Land Management's vast acreage holdings and control and the many lesser land-control programs such as the spider-web-like network of the federally-controlled highway systems. The danger to individual rights poised by the highway system is far more insidious than would appear at first glance. As recently as the first week in July, 1974, more than a million and a half acres in the Desert National Wildlife Range, which is controlled by the U.S. Department of the Interior and run by the Bureau of Land Management and by the Fish and Wildlife Service (see how the bureacracies intertwine?) was proposed as a wilderness area, which certainly sounds innocent enough. It even sounds ecologically oriented. The trick is that such a proposal would close these lands —a million and a half acres — to the public, with access *granted* only with written permission to certain mineral prospectors, which in itself brings to mind that part of the previous rule which deals with the cultivation of waste lands, etc. It is exactly such "harmless laws" and measures which are tightening an ever-smaller noose around our individual freedoms. Several years ago a plan was market-tested, via a daily newspaper, on the public's acceptance or rejection of a driver's pass system to gain access to the freeway/expressway system — which is a vital link in the federally-funded highway system. Unfortunately the public scoffed or ignored the idea, instead of being indignant and enraged at the proposed infringement upon their rights to move about unhampered. So that is another plan that is stored away until the moment it is needed. (8) Equal obligation for all to work. Establishment of industrial armies, especially for agriculture; (The well-heralded War-On-Poverty and it's many urban give-away centers and suburban or rural Youth Corps Centers are the latest in a more than four-decade test-program to get the American public to accept this concept. Remember the C.C.C. and the W.P.A. and the N.R.A. and the T.V.A.? The "harmless" forerunners to the current Youth Corps. They have all done their part in providing the needed research and development necessary to set a federally directed and controlled national work-corps into gear at the proper moment in history, as decided upon by certain leaders and spokesmen, but never voted upon by the American public in the manner devised by our forefathers.) (9) Combination of agriculture with manufacturing industries; Gradual abolition of all distinction between town and country by a more equable distribution of the population over the country; (The massive bulldozers of the many federally-financed Urban Renewal (removal) programs have very efficiently provided the initial models for urban population decentralization. They have thinned and spread entire inner-city core-groups into the poorly constructed federally financed F.H.A. suburban lo-density centers, and forcing the former suburban dwellers deeper and deeper into the countryside, in search of the sophisticated rural atmosphere they labor so diligently to obtain. The new owners soon realize that they, too, have been used and tricked, as the shoddily built units start falling apart at the seams because of inferior materials. Through this entire scenerio of dislocation, unhappiness, and misery, the F.H.A. maintains a cheery facade of well-meaning. They have after all, accomplished just what they set out to do, moving Americans from the urban centers into the surrounding countryside with a propaganda-eased efficiency that is seldom met in private industry.) (10) Free education for all children in public schools. Abolition of children's factory labor in its present form. Combination of education with industrial production, etc.; (The ever-increasing spectre of complete federal control of the public schools looms larger into reality with more and more federal say-so through the schools financial dependence upon educational subsidies, like the lunch programs, the many so-called "Title" programs, the busing programs, and at the higher level, the federally-sponsored community and junior college programs, which are heavily industrial-trade or technical-training-program oriented. From kindergarten through the post-graduate level, our schools are heavily dependent upon government funds. (2) It is a truism, "Who's bread I eat, who's song I sing.")

I chose to end this effort with this series of ten well-documented guidelines of power in order to illustrate how serious a state our beloved nation is in during this crucial period of my concern — the mid-nineteen-seventies. For those skeptics who will say, "So what;" let me hasten to state that those preceeding guidelines were not written by some ivory-tower leftist professor at some progressive university. Nor were these the goals motivating the sincere, if misled, forces behind the most recent defeat of McGovern at the polls. These premises are not even the secret and confusing guidelines of the recently deposed Nixon clique.

As I have mentioned many times throughout the book, it is now later than we think!! The ten precepts I have outlined in the preceeding paragraphs and pages are taken word for word — with nothing changed except my comments which were in the parentheses — from what is called the best and most accurate edition in the English language, translated by T. B. Bottomore, of the original text as written by Karl Marx and Friedrich Engels. Those ten rules or guidelines are the ten original planks of the communist manifesto — The basis for the foundation of communist governments internationally. The ten rules which the communist philosophy is founded upon are adhered to by our own federal government in practice. Go back and check them out, each of the ten has application to programs sponsored from the seat of our government in Washington, D.C.

I am not some radical-alarmist writing about some hypothetical bogeymen hiding under our national beds. I am a sane, rational, well-established businessman and entreupreneur, a viable and highly visable part of my community, who has taken the needed time and effort to amass some irrefutable facts about the state of my nation today. I am American-born and bred, with the proud American name of Houston, which is etched into the pages of American history and synonomous with Patriotism and heroism; and the brave blood of Sam

Houston flows in my veins, I am proud to say. The facts that I have amassed are available to all and sundry. But the vast majority of loyal Americans have been lulled into a false sense of "It-can't-happen-here" security, by those very forces that are causing it to happen here. I am attempting to awaken my fellow Americans in this book.

Who among us can deny that with some very basic arithmetic anyone can prove that a combination of income taxes, sales taxes, luxury taxes, gasoline taxes, utility and telephone taxes, property taxes, excise taxes, license fees, building fees and permits, business permit fees, and a whole host of hidden manufacturing-and/or-highway-use taxes and tolls and other fees, equals an end result that the great masses of the American public today pour seventy-three (73%) of our gross national productive income directly into the extravagant and waste-filled federal, state, and local governmental coffers? And to what end? The endless maize of boon doggling bureaucracy that seems dedicated to more and more give-away, free-spending programs that benefit no-one but the bureaucrats who so skillfully devise them.

We the people end up with just about one-quarter of our total productive income to service our needs, wants, desires, and savings programs. It seems to me something is gravely wrong in the basic economics of those proven figures. As a successful businessman with my areas of expertise in finance and economics and as an individual trying to make secure my family's position in our society, and as an individual attempting to enjoy some of the fruits of my own honest labors, that 27% to 73% ratio of sharing my personal economic pie seems a bit topsy-turvy and unbalanced, to say the least. I am on the short end of the sharing scale. You will note that I did not say my portion of any governmental dole, nor some state welfare subsidy, nor any local gift or handout. I am talking about the money which I sweated for and earned by dint of my personal preparation and industry. I am referring to my due rewards for my investments and my skills.

To look at it from another vantage point, what I am

doing is underwriting and subsidizing the entrenched bureaucracy and the creeping socialism it spawns. I am footing the bills to replace the old-fashioned labor-rewards-the-laborer system, with a one-for-all and all-for-one socialistic form of government which is anti-me and my best interests. I am doing all of these things with my capitalistic labors. That is closely akin to rewarding some-one to forcefully take away what I have earned and replacing it with a system of economic and mental servitude. I personally do not feel very prone to a servile mentality and I forcefully reject the idea that to question our government's current socialistic trends is to be less than patriotic. I feel that it is the highest form of pa-triotism to question elected officials and to make them answerable to the public. We have a clean cut choice my friends. Dress it up with a thousand fancy words and it still means the same thing. Big-brother slavery under communism or industry-rewarding freedom under our Republic as envisioned by our founding fathers. More directly, I am addressing myself to the question of whether you and I, and our children, and all future generations of Americans will be free people or will we be slaves? The words socialism and communism are totally interchange-able. Where the word communism is not acceptable, they use the word socialism. They are two sides of the same coin. Socialism is the pathfinder for communism. You will note that the birthplace of communism is officially titled the Union of Soviet *Socialist* Republic. Do you get my point?

One final point to show you just how this big-brother-ism is creeping into our land. Are you aware that if you move $5,000.00 in or out of your banking facility, that movement is now reported to the federal government. If you wish to take $5,000.00 or more out of the country, you now have to obtain permission to move, take, or ship your own personal property? Are you aware that the forces which would take away your freedom are constantly market-testing your attitudinal-acceptance quotient, and has been for many decades now? Already the limits of our repression/acceptance quotient have been carefully documented and filed away, awaiting only the proper time for implementation by these power-hungry jackals. Besides the expressway pass card system and the labor work pool tests (C.C.C., W.P.A., and etc.) that I have mentioned, the most recent test that I have noticed was a test statement by a high-ranking member of the current administration, proposing that we abandon the traditional "greenbacks" and adopt a new-look "red-colored" currency. Just stop and think about the symbolism of even the color they chose. Their reasoning for the red color was to remind the public that the federal government was operating in the red. That proposal was taken lightly by most, but it was and is a dead-serious test of the American attitude towards the changing of the currency.

"If business were run the same way Congress is, the country would have to shut down," says the first woman Congressional member from the state of Colorado, Ms Patricia Schroeder, a Phi Beta Kappa PhD leader of the future. (3).

So the attitudenal-acceptance testing continues on more and more fronts and concerning more and more areas of our lives. Many of us go blissfully about our way as though nothing serious was happening and the plotters note our apathy. The proposed red money is connected to the creeping socialism just as surely as the silent federal control of our communications and highway networks is a part and parcel of our lives today. I have quoted freely from other sources, concerned and otherwise, to substantiate that many charges I have made. I hope that you will check my references to be sure that I have stated my case correctly. My greatest hope is that many of you will read this book and that it will help awaken the masses of Americans to see the danger that is already here.

(1) *Time Magazine*—24, June, 1974, "The Lillian Ware Story'

(2) *Time Magazine*—15 July, 1974, Education, page 86

(3) *Time Magazine*—15 July, 1974, Leadership In America, page 62

The following Article was published in the May 1974
issue of the *Western Business News*

"A CREATIVE SOLUTION TO THE INFLATION DILEMMA"

by James Ray Houston

The following economic writers all agree that this country is facing a very severe economic dilemma. The
problem is well described by the titles of their books.
Harry Browne, author of "You Can Profit From A Mone-
tary Crisis," (now number three on the New York Times
Best Seller list); Harry Schultz, author of "Panics and
Crashes and How to Make Money Out of Them;" Wil-
liam Rickenbacker, author of "The Death of the Dollar;"
Harvey Peters, author of "America's Coming Bankruptcy;"
Robert Preston, author of "How to Prepare for the Com-
ing Crash;" along with the prestigious writings of Colonel
Harwood of the American Institute of Economic Research,
and the king of the gold bugs himself, Dr. Franz Pick of
London, England.

If you have read the writings of these men you will
have no difficulty understanding the dilemma facing the
economic policy makers of the U.S. Government. The
man most responsible for the financial mess the U.S. is
now in was a creative thinker by the name of John Maynard Keynes, creator of Keynesian Economics. The question is: was this mess created by accident, or by design?

In 1936 Mr. Keynes published his most important work,
"The General Theory of Employment, Interest and
Money." Just before publishing this book, Keynes wrote
to his friend George Bernard Shaw, the great fabian socialist and admirer of Stalin and Lenin and said, "To
understand my state of mind, however, you have to know
that I believe myself to be writing a book on economic
theory which will largely revolutionize . . . not, I suppose,

at once, but in the course of the next ten years . . . the way the world thinks about economic problems."* (From the book: Life of John Maynard Keynes by Harrod)

The basis of his creative idea was that government could print inflationary money at a very low cost and then place it into circulation through deficit spending and loans from the central banks.

By regulating the interest rate it could control the amount of money flowing into the economy thereby regulating the employment rate. Now to understand how this concept was going to "revolutionize" the world, we must refer back to something that Keynes wrote in 1920:

"Lenin is said to have declared that the best way to destroy the capitalist system was to debauch the currency. By a continuing process of inflation, governments can confiscate, secretly and unobserved, an important part of the wealth of their citizens . . . Lenin was certainly right. There is no more subtle or more sure means of overturning the existing basis of society than to debauch the currency. The process engages all the hidden forces of economic law on the side of destruction and does it in a manner which not one man in a million is able to diagnose."* (From the book, Economic Consequences of the Peace, John Maynard Keynes, pp. 235-236)

Keynes' entire "General Theory" is nothing more than a carefully disguised plan to break down the capitalist system.

The greatest tragedy is that President Nixon and his economic advisors thoroughly embraced Keynesian Economics as the official economic policy of his administration.

With this understanding I am going to try to state our present economic problem:

Due to socialist economic ideology (Keynesian Economics), this government has inflated the purchasing media of this country to the point of no return. Should we reverse the process and deflate the currency, an immediate ill-liquidity crisis would occur causing a deflationary type depression as bad or worse than that of the 1930's.

As you can readily understand, this would indeed be

harsh medicine for President Nixon or any politician to force upon the American people.

On the other hand, the consequences of continued inflation are even worse because of what happens to a nation when run-away inflation occurs. Run-away inflation is undoubtedly the worst thing that can hit a highly industrialized nation. Run-away inflation is always the final result of continued inflation. As soon as the currency has become totally worthless, the entire structure of our free market society would collapse overnight. According to Harry Browne, this is a very real possibility. In fact, he estimates the chance of run-away inflation in the U.S. as a 75% probability. The end result of this probability, would be the greatest and the longest depression we have ever known.

All of the aforementioned writers have articulated the problem well. Yet if you ask each of these men if anything can be done to stop the inevitable destruction of the currency, they would answer with a very definite "No." They claim that the process of inflation has progressed to the point where any effort to deflate the currency, and the automatic destruction of the purchasing power it represents, would set off a chain reaction of ill-liquidity that would result in depression.

At the risk of being contrary to popular opinion, I would like to propose what I believe to be a solution to this hereto insoluble problem.

THE DUAL MONETARY SYSTEM

The problem as I see it was caused by some very creative and unorthodox thinking on the part of John Maynard Keynes. Therefore could not some equally creative and unorthodox thinking produce an antidote? The answer would require finding some way to deflate the dollar without deflating the purchasing power that these dollars represent. The following is a proposal that I feel would do just that:

    The Government prints up a new currency. This currency however does not replace the dollar. In fact, it is not connected with the dollar in any way. This currency would be for grams of silver (31 grams per troy ounce). For example, a 100 gram note would not represent a fixed amount of dollars but would be redeemable at any time for 100 grams of .999 fine silver. There also would be notes for 10, 25, 50 and 1000 grams of silver.

Now the next question is, how would these gram notes get into circulation, and how would their value in the marketplace be determined? The answer to the first question is that U.S. Government would offer to sell U.S. silver grams to anyone who wanted to hold a currency that is redeemable for silver and would be free from depreciating effects of inflation. The selling price of a 100 silver grams note would be pegged by whatever the price of 100 grams of silver was selling for on the world silver markets. Its value in the marketplace would be the same.

With the value of the dollar depreciating daily, it would not be difficult for the Government to sell this currency to people who are now rushing to buy silver and gold backed currencies from other countries, and incidentally stop some of the flow into Swiss bank accounts.

The next questions are: (1) Is this silver currency backed by real silver and if so how does the government get it? Also, (2) wouldn't this cause a run out of the unredeemable dollar into the new redeemable silver grams, you know, "Gresham's Law" and all that?

The answer to the first question is that the government would take one-half of the paper dollars realized from the sale of the grams and buy silver on world markets. In effect, the government would have one-half of the silver backing the paper grams on deposit, ready and able to redeem any gram holders who desire redemption into real silver. The other half of the silver the Government would explain is in the mountains of California, Nevada, Idaho, etc., and the Government declares that should the demands for redemption eat up the ready reserves, it would take paper dollars and pay

110

miners to bring in the silver. Therefore, at least theoretically, each gram would be fully backed by silver.

In answer to the question about a run out of dollars into silver grams, the answer would be "yes" except for a special thing that the Government would do with the remaining half of the paper dollars left over after buying the silver. Remember, only one-half of the dollars were spent on silver. What would be done with the other half? Yes, you guessed it, they would be burned. As more and more people ran from the dollar to buy grams, more and more dollars would be destroyed. This, in effect, would deflate the currency. As more and more dollars were destroyed, the remaining dollars in circulation would become more valuable.

The buying of silver by the Government to back the paper grams would push the price of silver up to somewhere between $100 and $200 an ounce before the deflation of the dollar would stabilize its value. Thus, the run from dollars into grams would be stopped by natural market forces.

We would then have a dual monetary system with both kinds of currency in circulation. The dollar, a fiat currency, which is based on gold but not convertible into it, and the grams which are specie and would be backed by silver and convertible into it on demand.

There you have it. The answer to the problem of how to deflate the dollar without also destroying the buying power of the dollars destroyed. The purchasing power of the destroyed dollars would still be there in the form of grams. One of the advantages of this system would be its ease of implementation. A simple act of Congress is all that would be required and no one would be required and no one would be forced to do anything against his will. All the stability effects of the system would be caused by natural market forces as individuals seek to protect their own self interest.

However, this proposal presupposes that the Government admit its past sins and has a true desire to stop the inevitable destruction of its dollar. This is the only unrealistic part of this proposal.

111

ADVANTAGES OF THE DUAL MONETARY SYSTEM

1. Creates an alternate form of purchasing media that would still retain its value should the U.S. dollar collapse. This would save the basic structure of our free market society. This structure would otherwise disintegrate under run-away inflation conditions.

2. It would solve the basic problem of how to deflate the currency without a corresponding deflation of purchasing power.

3. There would be a slight re-distribution of the wealth to the many middle-class and senior citizens who have accumulated silver coins. For example: An elderly lady with $300 in silver coins would find that her coins would be worth approximately $20,000. (Estimated at $100 per ounce silver prices).

4. It stops the inflation of dollars. If this system is not enacted the run on silver will occur anyway as the inflated dollar continues to depreciate in value and sooner or later the price of silver will be one hundred dollars an ounce anyway. If runaway inflation occurs, it would go to one thousand dollars, or a million dollars an ounce.